The Skeptical Juror's Handbook

of Lawyers' Dirty Tricks

Steve Scarborogh

Genius
Book Publishing

The Skeptical Juror's Handbook of Lawyer's Dirty Tricks

Published by:
Genius Book Publishing
PO Box 250380
Milwaukee Wisconsin 53225 USA
GeniusBookPublishing.com

ISBN: 978-1-958727-80-5

250928 HQ

Contents

"Sure, it's my DNA, I was there, but they were already dead."

So You Are Now On A Jury

You've been summoned, appeared on your scheduled date, and sat through and participated in the selection process. You've been chosen to serve on a jury; it is time to get to work. You will listen to attorneys and witnesses, be presented with evidence, and be given at least two theories about how the crime was committed in your assigned case.

If your expectations to serve as a juror are similar to those you have watched on television, whether actual crime or fiction, your experience will most likely be vastly different. Sitting on a jury gives you a front-row seat to the action, and what you may encounter could be a game fraught with tricks and manipulations ranging from subtle to blatantly obvious to try to sway you, as the juror, from seeing the truth in the case you are being presented. This book can help guide you through all the ploys and maneuvers you could be bombarded with, so you can hopefully avoid being misled into a potential travesty of justice.

Some lawyers will try to confuse, hoodwink, and

misdirect you about the facts of your case. Let's get you prepared to be the best juror you can be!

In this book, you will learn about attorney gaslighting, the Rambo Lawyer, semantic infiltration, memory misattribution, bushwacking, belief speaking, SEDI and SOS, The hammer, hired defense witnesses, the CSI effect, and more.

Dispersed throughout these chapters are true crime examples of the topics presented. You will read about real cases that demonstrate the various themes and techniques used by lawyers in courtrooms throughout the U.S. It was difficult to wrap up this book due to the numerous instances of outrageous defenses that continue to occur. Be advised that although many of the true crime cases listed here are murders, many of the same defenses may be used by defense attorneys on cases of other crimes, from assault to grand theft or any crime that results in a jury trial.

The primary focus of this handbook is to expose the tactics and intentions of defense attorneys in their pursuit of a favorable outcome, regardless of the cost. It would serve you, the juror, well to remember that the prosecution team is also made up of lawyers, and they also want to "win" the case. Some of these techniques for winning may also be used by the prosecution lawyers. In some instances, the prosecutor has developed an intense relationship with the victims in the case and has an emotional connection to them. This may influence the type of tactics they use during the trial. You should be aware that the prosecution may use the same diversion tactics. You must be alert and vigilant when both sides present their cases.

Throughout this book, you will be presented with

some very outlandish defenses that defense attorneys have used for their clients. One way to think about this is that, regardless of the evidence in the case, the defense attorney must create a viable argument. That is their job. They're presenting you with what they've determined to be the best plan to try to get their client off and win the case, but that's not necessarily the whole truth.

A major perspective of this book is to show you all the dirty tricks defense attorneys may use during a trial, but this is not meant to prejudice you against defense attorneys in general. You should, of course, always listen carefully to both sides of the case. Some innocent people do get prosecuted. Listening carefully to everything presented throughout the trial is imperative to make the best, well-informed decision as a juror.

The jury system relies on people to put two and two together, extrapolate a conclusion from specific facts, and arrive at a sensible decision about an incident—a practical, unbiased view based on reviewing the information given to them during the trial.

Unfortunately, our American justice system today is based on an adversarial model that underlies the basic structure of the legal system, and that confrontation aspect is only one element of gamesmanship in play here in the U.S.

Most defense attorneys are honest and moral, guided by the principle of presenting the best possible defense for their clients. They fully ascribe to the axiom that everyone deserves proper representation. However, a jury member must still be vigilant and aware of the few unscrupulous defense attorneys out there.

The overall mission of a defense attorney is to create a defense that can convince a jury that their client is either innocent or that the prosecution hasn't proven their case. In doing so, some defense counsels may employ artful cross-examination techniques to disguise situations and attempt to deceive the jury into developing an inaccurate understanding of the facts.

Debate Team Mentality

In today's world, it is common that defense counsels take an immediate position on their client's side, no matter the guilt or innocence, and will present all the information from that side. It is almost as if attorneys are on a debate team. Take a point of view, no matter the real circumstances, no matter personal feelings or social principles, then argue that position. They may feel that their purpose is to present anything that supports their client, no matter the consequences or implications.

It is the art of the spin.

Trial by Jury

History

The right to a trial by jury played a significant role in sparking the American Revolution. In 1774, Founding Father John Adams said, "Representative government and trial by jury are the heart and lungs of liberty." Trial by jury is the only right that appears in both the Bill of Rights and the Constitution. That is how important it was to the first Americans. Colonists were not receiving proper trials from their British rulers, so, with this and other causes, the Revolution was underway.

Just as voting is essential to democracy, so is voting during jury deliberation essential to the right to trial by jury. Therefore, jury service is integral to the functioning of democracy. Regardless of the type of case, serving on a jury is a tremendous responsibility and crucial for our entire justice system.

It is unknown when the change from providing a

defendant with fair legal representation evolved into the sometimes anything goes presentation that includes lies, misdirection, and the gaslighting of jurors in today's legal world. We don't know precisely when it became acceptable for attorneys to lie to win their cases. Did this happen recently, or was it a slow erosion of attorney morality over time?

How did we get to this flawed system of justice? The best way to deal with this situation is to have jurors who are adequately prepared for courtroom antics and dirty trick tactics. This book should put you on the right path.

It may seem like there are a lot of criminal court trials occurring each year in the U.S., but of all the few thousand criminal cases brought against accused persons, it is estimated that only 2% ever go to trial. With this perspective, the few court cases that reach trial become particularly important. They change people's lives. You have that power.

Wouldn't you want someone like you on the jury deciding the fate of the accused, instead of someone who doesn't want to be there and perhaps doesn't care?

Overheard: "I sure hope I'm never in a position to have my fate decided by twelve people too stupid to get out of jury duty."

You may have heard the saying, "The only people on a jury were the people not smart enough to get out of it." That is not necessarily true; there are smart people on juries, too. The judicial system needs intelligent, discerning individuals who are willing to serve on juries.

People who can identify and fend off the dirty tricks thrown at juries by defense attorneys. People who are knowledgeable enough to analyze all the evidence and make a rational decision about the guilt or innocence of the defendant.

A juror should attempt to answer the significant questions of the case, like time frames, motives, and the validity of evidence, etc., and be able to sort through the games attorneys may play in order to find the truth.

In legal circles, it is common to hear the statement, "It is always a crapshoot with a jury," meaning that even with a slam-dunk case, you never know how people on a jury will react to the presentations. In a perfect world, that would not happen. The evidence should be straightforward, and conclusions easily reached. Unfortunately, that is not always the case. However, the deductions arrived from reviewing the evidence, those that lead away and those that lead toward the defendant, can also be deconstructed, if necessary, and the solid deductions will stand the scrutiny of your questions and deliver your conclusion to the case.

During the trial, the judge will decide the questions of law. You will decide the questions of fact. This means you are tasked with figuring out what really happened. Don't be surprised if the evidence given by both sides is conflicting or if witnesses contradict one another. After all, if there were no contradictions, and everyone knew what happened, there would be no need for a trial. That is when the real work begins for you, to weigh all the evidence and reach a conclusion about guilt or innocence.

Pretrial - Jury Selection

If you have already served jury duty, you may recall that during jury selection, you were asked many questions. This process is called *voir dire*. Voir dire is a term used to question expert witnesses, and it is also a term for a preliminary examination of potential jurors to determine whether they can be fair and impartial in the trial. This practice was designed for the lawyers to gain information about each potential juror and decide which ones they want to be on the jury. Those questions are designed specifically for that trial by the attorneys and perhaps by jury selection consultants. Both sides participate in the questioning.

If you made it to the jury, you answered the questions in such a way that you were accepted by the attorneys involved on both sides. Both sides also have a set of challenges to exclude certain people from serving on the jury, based on their answers to the voir dire questions. These are called *peremptory challenges.* These challenges are a lawyer's objection to a proposed juror, made without needing to provide a reason. The number of peremptory challenges allowed varies depending on the jurisdiction and the type of case. For example, in California, there are 10 peremptory challenges in criminal cases, 20 in cases involving the death penalty or life imprisonment, and 6 in civil cases.

Unfortunately, peremptory challenges can be another way to delay the trial. There can be a defense motion to grant more peremptory challenges. The motion can range from the total number of potential jurors questioned to the number of people questioned at one time.

It is typical for most states to require the court to screen the list of potential jurors to eliminate those who are unqualified or ineligible under state law, such as individuals with a felony conviction. There are also usually several exemptions that allow people to be excused from jury duty. Some jurisdictions permit exceptions for first responders, public officeholders, and active-duty members of the armed forces.

There is also a legal process of juror selection that is deemed "for cause." This is beyond the normal number of objections given by the judge. "For cause" means that the person is obviously so biased, so incapable of justice, that the judge can automatically reject them. And who would want them on the jury anyway?

You may also be selected as an *alternate juror*. Alternate jurors are chosen in some cases to replace jurors who may become ill or, for some other reason, cannot continue to serve through the entire trial. An alternate juror will hear all the testimony as the other jurors do, but they don't participate in the deliberations unless they replace an original juror.

Once you are impaneled as a juror, your role will be to listen to the evidence conscientiously and to try not to draw premature conclusions. The judge will instruct you not to discuss the case with outsiders or even with other jurors until deliberations.

Behind the Scenes Before the Trial - Judge Rulings

The judge on the case will oversee various pre-trial hearings and make decisions based on their application of the law.

These hearings are behind-the-scenes events that a juror never witnesses. These include motions, such as for a change of venue, exclusion of certain witnesses, and motions for more time to review the case.

Sometimes, these are merely tactics employed by defense attorneys before trial, designed to delay the trial or confuse the prosecution. An attorney may file any motion possible. They may throw everything they can come up with at the proverbial wall to see if any of them get the attention of the judge, and clog up the system.

Some of these motions may include requesting a delay in the trial dates, typically due to a need for additional time to review the case. Often, this technique is used when the case is especially damning to the defendant. A common mantra in lawyer circles is "If all else fails, delay, delay, delay."

There will usually also be evidentiary hearings, where the defense will challenge certain pieces of evidence for various reasons, such as violations of hearsay rules, improper search and seizure, prejudicial photographs, or specific reports. These may include a specific piece of physical evidence or might be an attempt to exclude particular witnesses from testifying on various grounds. These motions can be frivolous, and each takes time for the court to respond.

Among the most common defense motions is the motion to dismiss. This motion asks the court to dismiss the case because the defense thinks that there is not enough evidence to suggest that the defendant committed the crime, or that the evidence does not show that any crime has been committed. These motions may be submitted even if all the facts alleged by the prosecution are based upon a solid foundation. The judge must initially determine if a crime has been committed and if there is sufficient evidence to suggest that the defendant is the guilty party, thereby allowing the case to proceed to trial.

Additionally, motions to suppress evidence or witnesses can be based on almost anything the defense can conjure up, in the hope that the judge will be swayed. They are hoping to find a judge who will swallow their arguments and agree with the statements in their motions.

You may be aware of the motion to suppress a hearsay argument, such as information that someone was told but didn't experience. However, it can be common for the defense to make motions to exclude any piece of evidence in the case, especially evidence that is particularly damaging to their client. These might include personal diaries, phone recordings, text messages, and, especially, past criminal records.

These motions are usually related to matters such as the misuse of a warrant, evidence collected without a warrant, or failure to advise the client of their Miranda Rights. However, sometimes the motion to suppress may needle into small items within the case. In the O. J. Simpson case, the motion to suppress the slow-speed chase was granted because Judge Ito agreed with the defense that the Bronco chase was not directly related to the murders, and that the gun, the disguise, and the money within the Bronco did not necessarily mean that O. J. was trying to flee, was in despair over committing the crime, or that it was any admission of guilt.

All of this is done before the trial and is typically unseen by the jury. Lawyers often point out that "motions, motions, motions equal delay, delay, delay."

Grand Jury

A grand jury is sometimes convened before a person is charged or indicted for a crime. Grand juries are usually made up of about 15-25 members. This group of impartial citizens is tasked with determining whether there is sufficient evidence to indict someone for a crime. An attorney from the prosecutor's or district attorney's office usually leads the grand jury. Witnesses may be called to testify, and certain forms of evidence will be presented to the members. The prosecutor will then outline the case.

The grand jury listens to the witnesses and then votes in secret on whether it believes there is enough evidence to charge the person with a crime. Grand juries do not have an opposing attorney; only the prosecutor presents witnesses and evidence. There is no cross-examination of the witnesses. However, in some jurisdictions, members of the grand jury can ask questions of the witnesses.

If the grand jury chooses, they may decide not to charge the person of interest based on the evidence. All proceedings and statements made before a grand jury are sealed and kept secret. In some cases, a prosecutor or district attorney may decide not to proceed with prosecution even though a grand jury has recommended bringing charges.

In the Jon Benet Ramsey case in Colorado, a grand jury did recommend charges against John and Patsy Ramsey, indicating the jurors believed they placed Jon Benet in a situation resulting in her death, but the prosecutor nullified the findings of his own grand jury. Perhaps the prosecutor felt that the parents had suffered enough and that a jury would not have convicted them. This may account for the reason they were not at least charged with obstruction of justice.

It is interesting to note that the grand jury is a constitutional requirement for certain types of crimes and is even written into the United States Constitution. The general purpose of a grand jury is to have a group of citizens make an unbiased decision about the evidence presented by the prosecutor before voting to charge an individual with a crime.

Semantic Infiltration

Beware of semantic infiltration. Semantic infiltration is a deceptive ruse to change the words used in the case to confuse you and the jury by trying to minimize the harm the culprit did to their defendant. It is the use of a selected terminology to force someone to describe something in softer, milder terms to try to normalize horrible things or actions. "Then he just 'tapped' her, and she fell into the side of the glass table." Tapped is obviously less harmful than punched or even another weaker word, such as "slapped." He "accidentally" pulled the trigger. They "inadvertently bumped" into the victim.

This ploy is the attorney's process of relabeling potentially damaging terms to try to minimize the harm to their defendant.

The actual destructive and harmful use of semantic infiltration in a jury trial is accomplished by getting the jury to use the terms applied by the defense to the incidents in the case. This can be particularly dangerous in jury deliberations; jurors should use more general terms when making decisions and avoid those specific to the attorneys presenting their cases. You cannot let this gamesmanship taint deliberations.

Normalization

Another linguistic play that accompanies semantic infiltration is the pernicious use of normalization. While semantic infiltration involves the use of weak words, such as saying "bumped" instead of "smashed into," normalization is the repeated use of a horrible word in an attempt to make it seem normal or acceptable. An example might be the word "rape." The defense might use the word repeatedly so that it is no longer a jarring word, and the prosecution may use it to attack the defendant.

Opening Statements

On the first day of the trial, the attorneys will deliver opening statements. The opening statements are intended to tell jurors about the case they will be hearing and what each side will establish during the trial. The defense will introduce its primary defense. This is when you start building your evidence tower—the various points of evidence will be the imaginary bricks you use to complete your mental structure.

The prosecution will begin its opening statements, as it has the burden of proof, meaning it is responsible for proving the charge or allegation. The defense lawyer will follow with their opening statement. Either lawyer may decline to present an opening statement, and in some states, it may be possible for the defense to reserve its opening statement until the end of the prosecution's case.

A juror should pay close attention during opening statements. In most states, the opening statements must be restricted to facts that will be proved by the evidence and cannot be argumentative. A juror should keep track of all the assertions and defenses the defense attorney presents and retain those in memory or in notes for deliberations. If, during the trial, the defense does not present evidence of an assertion they made, or even implied, during opening statements, this should be a red flag for jurors.

During the Casey Anthony trial in 2011, the defense presented a supposition that it was possible that Casey Anthony's father, George, might have been abusive or had some possible participation in the cover-up or the death of his granddaughter, three-year-old Caylee. The defense even implied that Casey's seemingly detached behavior after Caylee's death was attributable to child abuse she had suffered at the hands of her father. During the trial, the defense never presented substantial evidence of either any childhood abuse of Casey or that George participated in a cover-up of any incident involving Caylee. This should have been a red flag to jurors that this was promised in opening statements but never delivered.

"We believe that a severe reaction to a tanning session caused her death."

During the opening statements, the defense may argue that the prosecution will not be able to prove, beyond a reasonable doubt, that the defendant committed the crime. You must be careful with such a statement that you can't prove something absolutely. This could be a semantic trap. The defense may say, "You may have a case with video and pictures of the defendant's car at the scene, driven by someone who looks like my client, but we can't be absolutely sure that they were the one driving it." As a juror, you are allowed to extrapolate, make inferences, and draw assumptions that make sense but may not be absolute.

During opening statements, it is possible that the defense counsel may blatantly misrepresent the law. They might do this by stating an incorrect summary of the written law for current cases. This may not be very clear for a couple of reasons. There may be multiple charges in the case, and there may be some subtleties with how the law is written in each instance. It may also be confusing because the layperson may not be familiar with the complexities of the law. It should be up to the other counsel to make an objection and correct the record if this type of deception and improper representation of the law occurs.

The defense attorney may even redefine the law to benefit their client, such as by altering the degree of theft or redefining the legal definition of assault and battery. This can be particularly confusing if various types of related charges are part of the case.

As a juror, you may ask the judge for clarification of the laws that pertain to the case. It is good practice to ask for this explanation.

The Appearance of the Defendant

There's also a very human element that we cannot suppress, and that is thinking in our minds, is this person in front of us, sitting at that table, capable of committing the crime they are accused of? They look so normal, like someone we know who is a good, respectable person.

Appearances, as we know, can be deceiving. How often have you seen pictures of a suspect when they were arrested, and then, when they appear in court, they look entirely different, much more presentable? Their hair is trimmed or carefully styled, and they are wearing conservative, business-like attire. Throughout the history of criminal justice, numerous cases have underscored the significance of a defendant's presence in court.

If the defense suggests that the person sitting in the courtroom is not capable of the crime, do not fall for that. The demure, maiden-like appearance of Lizzie Borden certainly contributed to her acquittal, as people at that time found it difficult to think that she could have done those wicked ax murders of her parents.

As a more recent example, Candy Montgomery, on trial in 1980 for the brutal ax murder of her friend, Betty Gore, and romantic rival for Betty's husband, presented very well in court. She wore conservative outfits, and her appearance was that of an everyday, ordinary housewife. Mrs. Montgomery was acquitted, possibly based on her contention of self-defense, but her appearance may also have influenced the decision in some way.

"It was self-defense, I had to shoot 'em that many times, unarmed or not."

A famous story, of which a book and movies have been made, is about Scotland Yard Detective Inspector Jack Whicher, who investigated the murder of a young child in the Kent family near Trowbridge, England. Inspector Wicher investigated the case and was sure that the young boy's teenage sisters had murdered him. The detective was not believed by society at the time, and he was ostracized within the police force because no one could imagine that these upper-crust young girls could have committed such a brutal crime. However, one of the sisters later confessed. Inspector Wicher was right all along.

Appearances, when it comes right down to it, mean nothing. A juror should suppress any emotional notions about the look of the defendant.

"We don't know the cause of death, so you cannot convict my client."

The Reputation of the Defendant

During a trial, a juror may hear the defense attorney attempt to restore the defendant's reputation after testimony that contradicts it and disparages their character. You may hear a defense attorney say that they agree their client is perhaps a bad person or a liar (if that has been established through testimony), but they will argue that this doesn't make them guilty of the crime they are being accused of.

Sometimes in a trial, especially one where the defendant has been portrayed as a person with a checkered past, that involved lying, infidelity, or violence, you may hear the defense attorney say, "I agree my client is a liar or a philander, and just not a nice person, but that doesn't make them guilty of this crime." In some cases, it can certainly make them appear guilty.

Do not let the defense confuse you by saying that just

because the defendant has a record, especially if it's a violent record, it doesn't mean they committed this crime. The defendant's past is certainly something you can consider. A pattern of behavior can be considered if there is testimony that the defendant has a history of being confrontational and hot-tempered. This would lend itself to being impulsive enough to commit the crime for which they are on trial.

Perhaps the defendant is caught in a lie. You may consider whether that lie is relevant to the current case. Were they lying about finances to their family, lying about their past, lying about their employment, or was it some lie intended to deflect from their involvement in the crime?

Suppose they're lying to deflect attention away from themselves and protect their interests. In that case, if infidelity plays into the crime, and if they have been violent in the past, these things should be considered, not dismissed, when deciding on the reputation of the defendant.

Similarly, the defense may suggest to you that the defendant could never have behaved in the necessary way to commit this crime. They might say, "They just don't have it in them," meaning this is not the type of person who would attack someone because of their civilized past. The defense may portray the defendant as a virtuous individual and have witnesses testify about their moral and wholesome character. The jury may hear that "they never could have done something like that." You should be skeptical of all the witnesses who testify that the defendant is a nice person. You surely have seen in the news the very normal-looking people who have been convicted of terrible crimes. You may even know someone who has surprised you with their behavior, maybe not by committing a crime, but they have betrayed you and have done some shocking things that you thought were beyond their typical personality. A juror should be aware of all the many, many cases where seemingly moral and wholesome people committed a crime completely out of character, such as in those examples mentioned above.

Think about the wives who have discovered that their husbands are serial killers. Their normal husband, whom they loved and who they raised their kids with, who had friendly barbeques with the neighbors, turned out to have brutally killed multiple people.

Alvin Bud Brown became linked through his DNA to two murders and was suspected by the police in at least four murders. He lived a quiet life in Portland, Oregon, with his wife, who was completely surprised when her husband was arrested and eventually sentenced to prison after being convicted of assault on a 15-year-old girl.

Hearing these personal circumstances and storylines, it will be very human and natural to feel some judgment toward the defendant. That is normal. While emotion is generally something to be suppressed by a juror, if these scenarios are well supported by testimony, you can make judgments about the personality of the defendant. You can extrapolate a person's personality and surmise their capacity to commit specific actions. This is a common occurrence in life and can also occur in jury deliberations.

Memory Misattribution

You should recognize that even when the witness genuinely believes what they are saying, there is a remote possibility that the witness has been overly coached and possibly even given planted information. This can be a deliberate misinformation process. This will occur more often with the prosecution, but it also happens with the defense.

One deceitful method through which the purposeful misinformation effect occurs can be called memory misattribution. This is where false information is suggested and then becomes incorporated into a person's memory of the actual event. An example of this would be a witness who, when questioned by investigators, heard the mention of a gun and that witness later says they saw the gun, even though their first statement did not include seeing any weapon.

An attorney can accomplish memory misattribution when interviewing a witness by making leading suggestions or completing sentences for them. They want the witness to "remember" things that help their case.

A juror cannot usually discern when this obfuscation occurs in the initial interview or subsequent interviews of the witnesses, but you can pick up on this technique during the testimony of a witness that may contradict previous evidence or witness testimony. Some clues include identical witness statements and testimony. If video or audio of the interviews was conducted, you may hear subtle leading statements by detectives.

Examples of leading statements include "When did you shoot him?" instead of "Tell us what happened next." Or "Did you see the knife?" instead of "What did you see?"

This memory misattribution has certainly happened in most of the repressed memory cases and in cases such as the Wenatchee child abuse case of the 1990s and the McMartin preschool child abuse cases from 1979, where witnesses claimed there was a basement where satanic sessions occurred. Witnesses appeared to have obtained information from other witnesses and police investigators that lent credence to the charges. All the charges were false, and there was no basement in that building.

You will want to resist being suggestible and maintain a firm account of the evidence delivered during the trial. You cannot allow the attorney to manipulate your memory and later use statements contrary to the previous testimony in the trial.

Prosecution Witnesses

Witness Questioning

Lawyers generally are prevented from asking leading questions of their own witnesses. Leading questions are those that suggest the answers the attorney wants, essentially prompting the witness to provide them. An example is, "Isn't it true that you saw Jack's cousin leaving in his car as you arrived at the scene?" This leads the witness to answer that they saw an alternative suspect at a particular place and time. The question should clearly have been, "What did you see when you arrived?" A lawyer should not put words in the mouth of the witness, because it is possible that the witness did not see the cousin but rather some unknown person driving away. Defense counsel can be very clever in phrasing the question in a way that elicits a specific answer. Hopefully, the opposing counsel will make the proper objections.

This is also a form of *skullduggery*, involving the use of leading questions that direct the witness to answer in a manner that favors the defendant. In these situations, a juror has to make the distinction between the questions and answers that have initially created objections and the following questions and answers. This can be especially important if the questioning happens in a flurry and the opposing counsel cannot keep up with their objections. It will be your task to determine where the attorney is asking leading questions or trying to put words into the witness's mouth.

Similarly, if a witness presents testimony that is stilted and sounds wholly memorized, it probably is. An extensively coached witness can be a manipulated witness. A defense attorney working with a witness to help them prepare for testimony always has the potential to skew the information in favor of the defendant.

In questioning a witness, another technique used by defense attorneys is to ask questions that require an explanation, but then attempt to limit the witness's answers to a simple yes or no. The defense attorneys compose these questions so that the witness's answer will create a false impression.

Another favorite underhanded trick of defense attorneys is to paraphrase a witness's testimony and modify it just enough to give the jury a significantly different impression of what they actually said. The attorney may say, "So what you're saying is…" or "To put it in other words…" or even, "Let me summarize your testimony…" If you hear these or any similar phrases, pay close attention to what they say next, and understand they may be changing the meaning of the witness's testimony.

Also, be aware of defense deceptiveness, which

involves expanding minor discrepancies out of proportion. Defense attorneys will sometimes focus on something insignificant that the witness did or did not do and blow it out of proportion to divert the jury's attention from the actual evidence. Certain questions about the crime scene, such as "What color was the carpet?" are used to misdirect. The answers may be insignificant, but the defendant's lawyer will make them appear to be of major importance.

A notorious example of this occurred during the O.J. Simpson trial. At one point, attorney Barry Scheck yelled about a suggested mistake by crime scene technician Criminalist Dennis Fung, who was on the stand for eight days, that in reality had a legitimate explanation and did not affect the discovery of the evidence in the case. Unfortunately, Mr. Fung became flustered and only meekly answered the subsequent questions.

Additionally, in the O. J. Simpson trial, considerable attention was drawn to the ill-fitting glove and the defense's statement, "If the glove doesn't fit, you must acquit." This could certainly fit into the category of defense courtroom antics. Upon reflection, there were many valid reasons why the glove wouldn't fit: a wet glove may shrink, the gloves were originally too small, or the person trying them on acted as if they didn't fit. The defense intended to direct the jury's focus to that particular piece of evidence so they might ignore the mounds of other incriminating evidence.

Do not always rely on the judge to keep a tight courtroom and disallow courtroom antics by the attorneys. Some judges will overlook this.

Statements such as "Did you know that..." are questions designed not to obtain information but to actually provide the defendant's perspective. They should not be given the normal weight of other testimony.

Additionally, questions that undermine a witness's credibility by attacking their character but are not otherwise relevant to the actual inquiry, especially without any application to the case, should be filed away in the "ignore" category. These have one purpose, and that is to mislead.

You should know that when the defense has a vital witness to question, and they think, "Uh oh, I must attack their background" to try to make them seem not credible, they are trying to poke holes in the testimony of the witness to protect their client.

Don't be gaslighted into thinking a witness is not credible because a defense attorney spends an inordinate amount of court time questioning that witness about their background. You may even give their testimony more consideration with the understanding that what they are presenting must be essential, or the defense attorney wouldn't be spending so much time on the questioning.

If the attorney commits some of these missteps, then receives an objection, and the objection is sustained (accepted) by the judge, resulting in a motion to strike the information from the record, it may be difficult to "unhear" specific statements. But you should do your best to disregard them.

Objections

During the trial, both attorneys can raise objections to the questions and questioning of witnesses. There should be a basis or grounds for the objection, such as the question is irrelevant, or that the topic is not relevant to the case. Another basis for an objection is that the question requests a response based on secondhand information that the witness heard or overheard someone else state. You may also hear the attorney object by saying that the question is speculative, the witness is being asked to speculate or offer a conclusion that is beyond the scope of the question or their expertise.

It should be noted that, even if the judge makes decisions on all objections against one attorney or the other, they are not taking sides or indicating to jurors how they should decide the case.

Scientific Witness Nullification

In the world of scientific testimony, do not fall into the trap of scientific witness nullification. Scientific witness nullification is another ploy, typically presented by the defense. This is when the prosecution presents a scientific witness to attest to, perhaps, DNA or fingerprints, and the defense presents its own scientific witness. Sometimes, the defense witness is called to provide a balanced perspective; however, the defense's intent is often to invalidate or nullify the prosecution witness's testimony. In witness nullification, the witness is positioned to get you, as a juror, to be so confused that you totally nullify and dismiss that testimony, and disregard that particular form of evidence and not consider it in deliberations. This is usually a win for the defense.

Another form of witness nullification occurs when the defense calls multiple technical or scientific witnesses to challenge a specific type of evidence. Multiple witnesses should not sway you. Even a whole battery of witnesses may all be stretching the truth.

The Rambo Lawyer

A lawyer known for continually using underhanded tactics during a case is referred to as a "Rambo Lawyer."

A Rambo lawyer is sometimes seen as conducting a "scorched earth" campaign, fiercely attacking the integrity of the witnesses, sometimes their own witnesses, and making insinuations that other people, perhaps the defendant's own family members, are the real culprits of the crime. This may have been what the defense attorney in the Casey Anthony case was trying to do when he implied that the defendant's father may have been abusive and may have been the real culprit in the case.

A Rambo lawyer can be classified as an attorney who is out to win the case at any cost. These types of attorneys may even file ethical or judicial complaints against the opposing counsel or the judge. Sometimes they make, in court or out of court, veiled threats against witnesses or even the judge. These threats typically have nothing to do with the details in the case but serve as a distraction.

The most egregious example of Rambo lawyering in a criminal case might be when the defense attorney implies that a witness supplying damning testimony against their client is actually a threat to the jury. This might occur when a witness has been charged with a crime or is a party to the crime in question.

Perhaps not quite in the category of Rambo lawyering, but another shifty tactic that some defense attorneys may use is to try to slip misinformation into the jury room through a press conference. The concept relies on statements made by the attorney to the waiting press, with the intention that the information will somehow reach the jury room through some juror, either intentionally or inadvertently, reading or hearing about the trial in the media. This trick is centered upon the counsel making a mischaracterization of a witness statement or a piece of evidence.

If it seems like your case involves a Rambo-type lawyer, you must decide whether an attorney's claims are principled or self-serving.

Evidence

What is Evidence?

All evidence is cumulative. It is the combination of all the information that leads to the conclusion reached by the jury. Evidence is presented to the court through the testimony of witnesses. They may be on the stand to explain police or examination reports, or they may explain exhibits such as photographs of evidence collected or enlarged photographs of the crime scene. All of these pieces will contribute to the mental evidence tower you are building.

There are basically two types of evidence, direct and circumstantial. Direct evidence relates directly to placing the criminal at the scene of the crime. In court, direct evidence includes testimony by a witness regarding what they personally saw, heard, or did. It includes firsthand observations, such as eyewitness accounts or footage from police dashboard video cameras. For example, a witness states that she saw a defendant pointing a gun at a victim during a robbery. Confessions are also considered direct evidence.

Circumstantial evidence encompasses physical and forensic evidence, such as fingerprints and DNA, as well as inferences, including alibis and motives. As a juror, you should know that there is often a common misconception about the definitions of direct evidence and circumstantial evidence.

A defendant can and has been convicted on purely circumstantial evidence, especially if the circumstantial evidence provides a preponderance of inculpatory evidence, evidence that shows or tends to show a person's involvement in an act.

You may hear the defense attorney say, "This is a circumstantial case; the defendant's mere presence at the scene does not mean he committed the crime and does not indicate guilt." This is an example of demeaning the concept of circumstantial evidence to favor the defendant.

The 2002 Lacy Peterson murder case in Modesto, California, is an example of a circumstantial evidence case. Substantial circumstantial evidence pointed directly to Lacy's husband, including the major fact that her body was later found in the San Francisco Bay within miles of where he admitted he went fishing on the very day she was reported missing, some 80 miles away from their home in Modesto.

The circumstantial evidence presented in the Rebecca Bliefnick 2023 murder case in Illinois, known as the Family Feud Murder, included pieces of video, fitness tracker records, tool mark similarities, plastic bag similarities, Google searches, and ballistic evidence. The ballistic evidence consisted of casings found in the defendant's home that matched those from the crime scene, as fired from the same weapon. All of those items were circumstantial evidence with a link to the defendant that made a convincing case. It is interesting to note that the defense attorney said, "[They] didn't find DNA, a hair, or fiber evidence, and the ballistic evidence was not necessarily reliable."

"No one saw him do it, no witnesses, so he didn't do it."

In the 2023 trial for the 2021 murders of Maggie Murdaugh and their son, Paul, in South Carolina, at first, the defendant denied being at the scene, but once a phone recording was discovered, the defense had to admit he was present. As a result, the defense was forced to state that "the state has proven at most that he was at the kennels at 8:44 p.m." The prosecution then presented evidence that this was almost exactly the time of the murders.

The defense called a parade of expert witnesses, including a crime scene engineer, a bloodstain spatter analyst, and a pathologist to dispute the damning circumstantial evidence presented by the prosecution. After less than three hours of deliberation, the jury found the defendant guilty of two counts of murder.

In addition to the other tactics covered in this book, one of the most important things to understand as a juror is that circumstantial evidence remains crucial and can be used to point to the perpetrator and convict the defendant.

Locard's Principle

In the world of forensic science, an early pioneer in the field was Edmond Locard. Locard's Exchange Principle states that contact between people and objects during a crime can involve a transfer of material that serves as evidence of the crime. This transfer can take many forms and accommodate most types of evidence associated with a crime.

Physical Evidence

Technically and legally, physical evidence is considered circumstantial evidence. Most physical evidence, except for fingerprints, which are unique, is considered class evidence, meaning it fits a group of items rather than a single specific item. Class evidence, however, can narrow down the possibilities of mere coincidence. A paint chip from a specific manufacturer and model of car is a form of class evidence. Even though that paint chip could belong to an entire group of cars of that model and color, if the subject has that type of car, then that should be included as part of the circumstantial evidence that links to the subject.

Biological evidence, such as human hair, is circumstantial evidence that can significantly narrow down the group of suspects or even identify a likely individual, which can be highly persuasive in court.

A juror should pay strict attention to any piece of evidence that is introduced, then is objected to, and then the objection is sustained or accepted by the judge, so it cannot be introduced. That dirty trick is sometimes known as legal prevarication, though most of the time, evidentiary hearings are not held in the presence of the jury. If this is done in front of the jury, it can be a ruse to partially present some evidence by the defense, to get it on the jury's mind. Much like when a statement is made by an attorney that is ultimately deemed to be stricken from the record by the judge, it can be damaging because the jury has already heard it.

"There is no physical evidence, DNA, or fingerprints linking the defendant, so he must be innocent."

Evidence Awareness - The CSI Effect

A juror should be aware of the CSI Effect. This is the perception that there will always be a large amount of physical evidence at a crime scene. On TV shows like CSI and in the movies, crime scenes are loaded with evidence. A typical crime is not like that. Not every crime scene produces copious amounts of physical evidence. Latent prints are not always found. DNA is not always available. Sometimes, ballistic material, such as bullets, cannot be matched to a specific weapon.

Not every surface allows for the transfer of fingerprints or DNA. Fingerprints are essentially delicate and consist of the moisture and oils produced by human skin. Most handguns are designed to resist fingerprints. The surface is manufactured to repel damaging skin oils, thereby protecting the surface.

Bullets, especially those that collide with bone, are sometimes damaged so severely that they cannot be ballistically compared to other bullets. This means that sometimes bullets can only be typed for caliber and provide no additional evidentiary value.

A juror should remember that just because fingerprints are not found, DNA is not recovered, and the weapons cannot be determined, it does not mean the defendant is innocent. If the defense attorney makes that implication, it should be regarded with skepticism. The absence of evidence, in most cases, should not be considered evidence.

Fingerprints can be damaged by the simple movement of the hands or even the gloves of a crime scene investigator, but once they are processed by photography or chemical means, they are considered solid evidence. No two fingerprints are alike, no matter what a defense attorney might imply.

Additionally, a defense attorney may argue that because many people handled an item from which a fingerprint (identified as belonging to their client) was recovered, it should be considered invalid. This is not true, by any means. This tactic was presented in the Hall-Mills case, a double murder in the 1920s New Jersey, where a small calling card (business card) was processed, and a fingerprint of one of the suspects was recovered. The defense's approach in that case was that, since many people had touched the card, the suspect's fingerprint should be discounted. This was not a practical defense and should have been rejected because it doesn't matter if many people touched the same object; if a fingerprint is recovered, it means that person touched that object. Many people can touch an object without damaging or altering fingerprints. The defendant in the Hall-Mills case was acquitted, possibly due to this misunderstanding.

If fingerprints are introduced during your criminal case, do not let the defense suggest in any way, shape, or form that fingerprints are anything less than unique. A subversive set of lawyers have proposed, based on, it seems, a philosophical approach, that fingerprints could possibly be duplicated somewhere, somehow. This is hogwash and should not be given any credence. There is no scientific basis for this suggestion and all scientific evidence—in fact, all biological, astronomical, earth science, and the natural sciences—show us all the vast uniqueness in nature. Even identical twins have different fingerprints. Fingerprints are and will always be unique to an individual person. The defense may state that because DNA was not recovered, even though a perpetrator had to have touched certain items at the crime scene, either the case was botched, or it proves his client innocent. "My client was not matched to any DNA, so he could not have committed the crime." This supposition is not correct. DNA is not always recovered at crime scenes. To transfer DNA, body fluids, such as blood, sweat, or semen, must be deposited on an object or surface at the scene. The CSI unit or forensic chemists must then be able to locate this usually invisible substance and collect it. They may not have swabbed the exact surface or area, or there may have been something like weather that allowed it to be deposited but not collected. Because DNA was not recovered, it does not mean that the defendant did not commit the crime.

Conversely, if DNA is recovered but does not match the defendant, it does not make them innocent. There are a myriad of reasons as to why this could have happened. It can be simply other people with access to the crime scene area who are unknown and uninvolved in the crime. For example, the DNA recovered from Jon Benet Ramsey's underwear may be that of the factory worker who packed the new set of clothing. In Europe during the late 1990s and early 2000s, it was believed that one person was committing crimes throughout the continent. However, it was finally determined that one worker at a cotton swab factory had contributed the DNA.

Questioning Evidence

In the Rebecca Bliefnick murder case in Quincy, Illinois, police found multiple shell casings at the scene. Police then later recovered many, many more shell casings in her ex-husband's house. Ballistics analysis showed that the same gun fired the casings at the murder scene as those found inside the defendant's home. The defense presented an argument that the murder gun wasn't found, so "we don't know for sure if the defendant committed the crime." When evidence is questioned during the trial, it is sensible to weigh both the presentation of the evidence and the validity of the defense's response. If it sounds absurd, it probably is.

As a juror, you will be asked to pay attention to small

things and put them all together to develop a theory about how the defendant did it, but often during a trial the defense attorneys might ask you to focus on one *small* thing such as an inconsistency in the time frame, and ask you to use that irregularity to dismiss the whole case against the defendant. It is always the total of all the evidence put together that makes the case. Remember that you, as the juror, have the authority to give weight and counterweight to each piece of testimony and evidence.

In some cases, even eyewitness testimony should be taken with a grain of salt. Especially if the witness is recalling something that happened years prior, or the way they arrived at their memory was questionable.

In a case of a person becoming both the defendant and the victim, George Franklin was tried in 1990 and convicted of the murder of a little girl who was a friend of his daughter. Though there was no physical evidence, Franklin was convicted based on a recovered memory. Twenty years later, Franklin's daughter "remembered" that her father had committed the murder. The young witness's mother even began doubting the recovered memory of her daughter. The daughter's "memory" also came into doubt when she accessed memories of other murders her father had committed. Franklin, after spending six years in jail, was eventually exonerated; another man was convicted of the murder, and the psychotherapy technique of recovered memories was discredited.

Variances and Possible Versions of the Crime

Unfortunately, for many criminal cases in the justice system, there will always, always be variances that arise. The timelines may not be absolutely exact, alibis cannot be verified, or there may have been sloppy police work, but this should not mean that you dismiss all the other evidence presented in the case. Some doubts about specific forms of evidence do not invalidate all the evidence in the case.

Real life is not like in the movies; real crime is not so neat and clean. Criminal cases will always be murky, puzzling, and complicated. There will invariably be loose ends. There may be an unaccounted fiber or hair, some unknown blood spots, or even an unidentified random fingerprint. It is essential to keep in mind that all evidence is cumulative. It is always the total of the evidence, perhaps despite some inherent inconsistencies, that points to the actual perpetrator.

One way for a juror to look at discrepancies or specific issues brought up by the defense is to analyze all the other evidence. Go ahead and set aside that particular issue, but evaluate the other evidence provided by witnesses and decide if there is still enough evidence. Then put that discrepancy back in and see if it significantly sways your conclusion.

It is also essential to understand that there can be other versions of the crime than that presented by the attorneys in the trial. The nature of crime is that one can almost never know the exact circumstances of the incident, or even remember it perfectly, even if they were there at the time. Sometimes, even the perpetrator, due to a psychotic or altered state, may not remember all the facts. The prosecution may present a version that they believe fits the facts, even if it does not precisely match the facts, but that should not lead to the automatic dismissal of all the evidence presented.

Smoking Gun

You must know that it is very, very rare that there is a proverbial "smoking gun" in criminal cases, a clear piece of evidence or an eyewitness to the crime. In fact, "smoking gun" cases usually don't even go to trial. In those cases where there is clear evidence pointing specifically to one person, that person will usually take a plea. They know that they will be found guilty and will have pleaded to obtain a lesser amount of jail time or to avoid the death penalty. A jury will rarely even be seated in most "smoking gun" cases. However, sometimes there is the obviously guilty defendant who thinks they can beat the justice system. Their expansive ego will not let them plead guilty, even if the case is a "slam dunk."

"Smoking gun" cases that do go to trial are typically those where the defendant refuses to plead to any lesser charge or any charge, with the assumption that they can beat the allegations. It may be a narcissistic individual who thinks they are smarter than any judge or jury, that no matter the quality or amount of evidence, they will not be convicted.

Some defendants believe they are special with special privileges and are entitled to be above the law. They think that they can do anything without any consequence because of who they are, and that a jury will not dare convict them of a crime.

The 2011 case against a former police officer in the murder of Jennifer Webb in New Jersey would fit the category of a "smoking gun" case. There was a mountain of evidence, including multiple DNA confirmations, that led directly to the perpetrator. The defendant was convicted in 2012. In a hindsight assessment, the O.J. Simpson case and the Steven Avery case would easily fit as "smoking gun" cases due to the vast amounts of inculpatory evidence.

Minimizing Important Evidence

A common subtly deceptive tactic is to try to minimize significant evidence that is especially damning. Evidence such as fingerprints, DNA, video, or firearms testing is extremely important to a criminal case. It is, of course, a good tactic for the defense to minimize that type of evidence. If the defense can neutralize particular types of evidence or make it seem less important, then it is possible that the jury will not focus on it.

A common approach for an attorney to take is to refrain from questioning a witness who is presenting scientific evidence. With a dismissive expression, the defense attorney may say, "No questions for this witness, Your Honor." This technique implies that the witness has no significant impact on the case.

Defense attorneys can also minimize the impact of specific evidence by describing it effectively during the trial or in their opening statements and summations.

In the 2022 cyclist Anna Moriah Wilson murder case in Austin, Texas, prosecutors presented video, cell phone, ballistics, and DNA evidence. The defense claimed that there was no video of the defendant at the scene and that the DNA science was questionable, saying, "No camera footage showed her at the scene." However, Kaitlin Marie Armstrong, a rival for the affections of a fellow cyclist, was convicted of the murder and sentenced to 90 years in prison.

Another example of this tactic occurred in a driving accident in Malibu, California. The police said the GPS clocked the driver at 90 mph in a 45 mph zone. The defense in this case stated to the press that his client was only driving 70 mph.

Time of Death

In murder cases, the time of death, TOD, is often very important. One thing to remember about the time of death is that a coroner or pathologist should almost always frame their conclusion as an estimate.

TOD can be difficult for a coroner or medical examiner to establish. The only absolutely accurate determination of the time of death is the uncommon circumstance in which a person died with a qualified medical professional present. You may have heard of rare cases where a pacemaker tracked the time of death or a victim's watch broke, but even these are sometimes inaccurate. Therefore, TOD should not be considered concrete when pinning down alibis.

In many homicides not committed in public, the perpetrator is typically the only surviving witness. This means that when the medical examiner determines the time of death, they can only estimate an approximate time.

However, a reliable estimation of the TOD can lead to discovering the identity of the assailant. In criminal cases, it can eliminate some suspects while focusing attention on others. All the alibis of the persons of interest in a case can be scrutinized based on the estimated TOD.

Suppose an attorney purposely states a more restricted timeframe than the estimated TOD provided by the medical examiner. In that case, this can be considered deceitful manipulation, as the intent is most likely to suggest that the defendant could not have committed the crime.

Method of Death

In some cases of murder, due to the condition of the body, the specific method of death cannot be determined. Method of death is also known as the cause of death (COD).

If the COD cannot be determined, it should not be considered exculpatory evidence and should not be used to exonerate the defendant. If the defendant was the last to be with the victim, and it can be proven that they were with the victim just before they were killed or attacked, even if the COD cannot be determined, the defendant should not be automatically acquitted.

The COD seemed to be a major factor in the jury's decision in the Caylee Anthony case. Despite the presence of duct tape on or near the body, the defendant being with the child before her disappearance, the suspicious odor in the defendant's abandoned car, the discovery of the body in close proximity to the defendant's home, and a plethora of proven lies, the defendant was acquitted.

If there exists a substantial amount of evidence pointing directly to the defendant, an absence of COD should not be given overwhelming weight.

Bushwacking

"Bushwacking" is a term that can be used to describe an attorney presenting information about the case

outside of the record and not within the confines of the trial. The term is particularly appropriate when a trial attorney resorts to their own assertions of fact without the opportunity for the opposition to pose objections or test the evidence through cross-examination.

Bushwacking can also occur when the attorney provides their personal understanding of the facts in the case, from only the defendant's perspective, usually in press releases.

Bushwacking is also a method of trying to taint the jury pool. Talking to the press and presenting a slanted side of the case can be a trick to skirt the court and judicial process, and to try to taint the minds of possible jurors.

This is especially devious when the talking points would probably be subject to vehement objections and never admissible. The defense attorney can attack the victim's reputation, discuss questionable evidence that may not be admissible in the trial, and even attempt to create bias against the prosecution or the judge.

In the 2022 Courtney Clenney murder case in Miami, the prosecution asked for the court to impose sanctions on the defendant's attorney after the counsel made dehumanizing remarks about the victim during press conferences.

Chain of Custody

Chain of custody refers to the tracking of a piece of evidence from the point of collection to storage, through analysis, and back to storage. Sometimes something abnormal can happen in a tracking system. Things are misplaced, signatures are missing, or packaging is compromised, among other developments. None of this should necessarily mean that a chain of custody was broken. It can just mean that there were issues with tracking the evidence.

If the defense uncovers, during testimony, that the chain of custody for certain items of evidence is compromised and implies that the chain of custody is "broken," you might want to make sure it is a significant factor. A disruption in the chain of custody does not automatically mean that the evidence should be disregarded; however, it may necessitate further investigation. It especially does not mean that other evidence in the case should be dismissed. Other forms of evidence can still be considered, and if the remaining evidence is still convincing, it can be used as part of the compilation of evidence in the case.

In the 1986 cold case killing of Ruby Doss in Spokane, Washington, a DNA hit was linked to a suspect. During the 2015 trial, the defense argued that the evidence was contaminated due to the disheveled appearance of the packages containing the defendant's DNA. Essentially, they were arguing that the chain of custody for the item was broken, and therefore, the evidence should be excluded. There are two key points to remember in cases like this. One concern is that evidence packaging can be damaged, especially in cold cases, which may even suggest a "broken" chain of custody; however, this does not automatically mean that the evidence should be disregarded. Additionally, it is impossible to contaminate DNA and alter it to resemble someone else's DNA. DNA might be too diluted to assign to a particular individual, but it cannot be changed into another person's DNA.

No Body

There may be a murder case where there is no body of the victim that has been discovered, but the prosecution still believes that the victim is deceased, based upon several conditions such as a copious amount of the victim's blood discovered at the scene, the victim's abandoned car (perhaps with blood located inside), no cell phone or banking activity for many months or years, no contact with relatives or friends, and of course no confirmed physical sightings of the victim.

Think deeply if there's no body and the defense suggests the missing person may still be alive. The defense may be that because no one has found the body, the person is still living; therefore, the defendant cannot be charged with murder. It may be beyond belief to consider that after weeks, months, and years of being missing with no contact, no cell phone signals, no banking or credit card use, the person is still alive. It would be a rare situation where a person escapes from their family and leaves absolutely no trace of their whereabouts. This is especially true if there were children, siblings, or other family members present in the missing person's life.

And remember, there will always be "sightings" by people wishing to help. Realize that in missing persons cases, there are as many as hundreds of sightings that are called in to the police. Many of these, incidentally, report clothing that is vastly different from what the person was last seen wearing, often in locations impossible for the person to have reached within the given time frame.

In the Laci Peterson murder case, missing person reports came in where people thought they saw the victim on the day and days after she was reported missing by her husband. Tips were reported that had Mrs. Peterson walking a different breed of dog, wearing entirely different clothing, in an area far away from the park where she was said to have been last seen walking her dog. Witness sightings are often unreliable.

A "no body" case should not be automatically dismissed, and all the evidence should be carefully analyzed.

"There is no body, we don't even know if they are dead."

Alibi

You have undoubtedly heard the term "alibi." An alibi is a defense claim that a person was elsewhere at the time of the offense or could not have physically done the act. An alibi is essentially an excuse for why they couldn't have done it: They were somewhere else at the time of the incident.

Sometimes the alibi offered by the defense appears very solid, but it does not seem to cover the entire time of the occurrence. Sometimes the alibi of the defendant may follow along the lines of "I was at home, alone, asleep," with nothing concrete to oppose that statement.

If there are any holes at all in the defendant's alibi, you might give it extra weight—the same for any doubts about the exact times of the defendant's whereabouts. An alibi should not be automatically accepted, even when it is presented as being very firm. The best alibis are often reinforced by witnesses or physical evidence, such as CCTV (closed-circuit television) or video evidence.

Staging

In some cases, you may come across something that the detective or crime scene investigator describes as staging. This is where certain aspects of the crime scene have been arranged to create a form of misdirection. Parts of the scene were created to give investigators the impression of something different than what really happened. Staging, you might be familiar with, is when someone has pulled out the drawers in a home where a murder has happened to give the impression that the case was a burglary gone wrong. Another example might be when a victim's wallet is taken in order to make a purposeful assault seem like a mugging.

If there is any staging, there must be a reason for that deception. Staging is always an attempt to deflect attention away from the real culprit. The purpose of staging is first to disguise the crime itself, then to deflect attention away from the real perpetrator.

Staging is another form of lying, except that it is done

with physical items or implications instead of words.

There were multiple examples of apparent staging in the JonBenet Ramsey murder case. The suitcase under the basement window suggested an exit by an outside suspect, even though the front door was right by the basement stairs, a door one would have to pass to go up to the child's room, and an easy exit resembles staging. The garrote, fashioned by craft items from within the house (to account for the strangulation), and an extensive handwritten three-page "ransom note" (written on family stationery) with all kinds of hints pointing to some supposed politically motivated kidnapping group, also smacks of staging.

Similarly, there was apparent staging observed in the Sam Sheppard case in 1954, so much so that it can't all be listed here. One example was the drawers from a writing desk that appeared carefully laid out on the study floor, but nothing looked to have been disrupted within the drawers, unlike in a typical burglary. Then, Sheppard's medical bag was opened, and some medical items were spilled on the floor, implying a burglar looking for drugs, but it was all just too neat. A green bag containing some valuables was found in the backyard, suggesting it had been dropped from a high bluff leading toward the lake, rather than the street.

Additionally, in the Sheppard case, the position of Mrs. Sheppard on her bed was also suspicious. If the staging was to suggest a sexual assault, it was not well thought out since the crossbar of the four-poster bed was blocking any attempt at sex.

A final issue with staging is that it is highly subjective,

and without being in the mind of the perpetrator, it is impossible to precisely understand what they were thinking at the time of the incident.

If you are confronted with a case where staging is suggested, pay close attention to the details, and decide for yourself if it seems like the particulars are indeed staging with a purpose of misdirection.

Coincidences

Many prosecution cases encompass the connection of many links that lead directly to the defendant. The defense may present a case that rests on the premise that all those coincidences were just happenstance. They may propose that the coincidences, no matter how many, were unrelated. That they were just accidental flukes.

An example might be a statement by the defense that it was just a coincidence that a car of the type the defendant drives was seen at the crime scene around the time of the incident, and his phone pinged on a nearby tower at that time; however, the defendant claims he was not there.

The defense would have you believe that many coincidences just happened to occur in the Scott Peterson case. On the day of his wife's disappearance, he just happened to go to his storage unit, where he made some anchors, picked up his boat, and then went fishing very near where his wife's body was eventually recovered.

"They slipped and fell and hit their head. It was an accident. So, I had to..."

A defense attorney may tell you that the defendant buying cleaning supplies right after the crime is a coincidence. That it is a regular occurrence. We all buy cleaning supplies from time to time. But is it really normal? Suppose a defense attorney excuses the purchase by the defendant, usually on video at a Walmart or similar place, of various cleaning supplies, including bleach, a mop, and ammonia, as just a coincidence. In that case, you may want to give it the weight it deserves, especially if the prosecution presented evidence that some cleanup was done at the crime scene.

Or maybe there is a presentation of the purchase of lye and shovels in a case when the victim was buried. You may want to give it the necessary weight and not dismiss it as a mere coincidence.

In the 2023 Makayla Fay Meave murder case in Oklahoma, her husband was arrested for her murder. Records from the case show that the husband's work boots "had a blood-like substance on them" that investigators then stated came back as a positive DNA match to Makayla. And, according to court records, detectives also found a Walmart receipt for a mop, ammonia, and bleach purchased the day Makayla was reported missing. All these items were found on the husband's separate property. Of course, it was suggested that these purchases were mere coincidences.

Veteran detectives subscribe to the motto that "there are no coincidences." At least, not multiple coincidences that all point to the accused's guilt.

Gaslighting

Sometimes, one of the dirty tricks a defense attorney may practice during a trial is the use of gaslighting. Gaslighting is when the defense is trying to convince you that your perceptions of the evidence are wrong. That what you hear or see is different, a new interpretation of the facts. They may imply an alternate reality over and over again during the trial to the point that you begin to question what you believe to be true.

The defense attorney may attempt to get you to question reality or the facts in order to gain control and persuade you to side with their client. Gaslighting is about control. The control of your mind to get you to accept their defense in the case, to confuse you about what you think has really happened during the crime.

An example of gaslighting is an instance where the defense provides an interpretation of a witness's testimony that differs from what was actually said. Don't be gaslighted by the defense when they try to make something horrible seem normal. Don't be gaslighted when the defense implies that it is normal to panic and dispose of the body or to panic and continue shooting or stabbing the victim. That should not be an excuse for their actions.

The defense attorney may do this with witness testimony or by interpreting the value or weight of evidence. Some verbal tactics that a defense attorney may employ include misstating what the witness has just said or said earlier, or even misquoting what a witness previously stated to the police.

Gaslighting can be done in very subtle ways by just slightly changing the actual words of a witness when repeating what they said, in an attempt to create an alternative reality. A juror should carefully monitor the statements of the attorneys and not let them create a reality that slants the truth.

Similar to Semantic Infiltration, but usually done only once, an example of this tactic might be when the defense attorney restates a witness's statement about the defendant forcibly shoving the victim to the ground by saying, "And then you saw the defendant slightly bump the victim, right?" Or the many cases where the defense attorney rephrases the defendant's shooting the victim as "So that's when the gun accidentally discharged, unintentionally hitting the victim."

Cross Examination

CROSS-EXAMINATION IS THE QUESTIONING OF THE other side's witnesses. Cross-examination entails focusing on the substance of the witness's previous answers and attempting to correct the record if any discrepancies are found.

While not typically proper during initial or direct witness questioning, it is generally accepted that leading questions may be asked during cross-examination, as the purpose of cross-examination is to test the credibility of statements made during direct examination. The attorney can ask leading questions because the witness was not their witness, and they may resist any suggestion that what they say is not true.

Cross-examination is typically conducted to elicit answers from the witness that contradict their initial statements. An example of this type of questioning would be to elicit information where a defendant initially said they were never at the crime scene when subsequent information, such as phone GPS, shows otherwise, or they had stated that they never had intimate relations with the victim when DNA proves that they did.

Cross-examination is often used to suggest that the witness is lying or mistaken about what they saw or heard, particularly with witnesses who are there to provide an alibi for the defendant at the time the crime occurred.

Rebuttal Questioning

After the prosecution and the defense have presented their witnesses, each side can present rebuttal witnesses or evidence to counter prior evidence presented. They can put on new witnesses or recall witnesses who have already testified to refute the testimony of the other side's witnesses. This is a time for rebuttal only, and in most jurisdictions, attorneys are prohibited from presenting new witnesses or new evidence not previously admitted to the court. All witnesses must be included on the established witness list, and all evidence must be presented to the defense in what is known as "discovery" prior to the trial. Also, rebuttal witnesses must only address testimony previously submitted in the trial.

Forget what you have seen in the movies or on TV. Evidence uncovered at the last minute by a special investigator is rare. And when it does happen, it is rarely admitted into the trial. A new witness must be approved by the judge after discussion with the attorney, who must present their reasoning for their admission, and after the opposing attorney is given an opportunity to present reasons for not including the evidence.

Coaching Witnesses

You should recognize that a defense attorney can coach, direct, and maneuver a witness to benefit their client. Some guidance and preparation before a trial is normal, but pay attention if the questioning is so specific and controlled that it leaves you with unanswered questions. Hopefully, the prosecutor will address those concerns during cross-examination.

Look for clues that a witness's testimony is too rehearsed to the point of appearing to be memorized. They may even backtrack in their responses to "correct" their testimony, seemingly remembering what they meant to say. Remember, as a juror, you decide the weight you give to each witness.

The Hammer

There is an old legal adage that says, "If the facts are against you, hammer the law. If the law is against you, hammer the facts. If the facts and the law are against you, hammer the table [the opposing counsel]." This axiom may also apply to "hammer the witnesses."

Sometimes, the practice of hammering the opposing counsel or the prosecutor is done not in court but outside the courtroom, typically in press conferences. The attack may be on the prosecutor's motiva-

tion, implying that the indictment, investigation, or prosecution is biased against the defendant.

Hammering the witness means attacking the witness if the facts the witness is presenting are against you. This may be a position that the defense attorney takes for a witness who has testimony that is expected to be damaging to the defendant.

If all of these avenues have been exhausted, it would be folly to carry this adage further and hammer the judge, knowing that certain rulings will surely affect the case. However, this is usually done outside the courtroom, as it would surely be foolish to attack a judge in open court.

(The original quote about the hammer is attributed to poet Carl Sandburg and ends with "pound the table.")

Reputation Attacks on Witnesses

You should be aware that during cross-examination, attorneys may attempt to question the witness's ability to recall and accurately describe their experience, or to *impeach* the witness. Impeach, in this sense, means to question or discredit. The purpose of impeaching a witness is to lessen the impact of the evidence they are presenting. A notion among attorneys is that if a witness has damning information, attack the witness themselves.

One way an attorney might attempt to impeach a witness is by demonstrating prejudice or bias in the witness, such as their relationship or friendship with one of the parties, or their interest in the outcome of the case. The attorney can ask questions that imply the witness will benefit in some way if the case goes in a certain direction. This may be true; however, the witness may still be telling the truth.

Because sharp, attacking cross-examination is a powerful tool in the courtroom, pay attention to what could be categorized as reputation attacks or attempts to degrade the character of a witness solely to weaken their testimony.

An attorney may use some underhanded techniques to accomplish this, and you will need to be able to sort out the testimony from the attack to make sure the attack is warranted. An example might be accusing a witness of lying without providing any evidence to substantiate their claim of untruthfulness. This can be accomplished by an attorney when a witness is not sure about their testimony or hedges on certain facts. In reality, the witness may be hesitant and not want to present evidence in a way that implies a particular conclusion.

On the other hand, the witness may have lied. It is quite ironic that the defense is condemning that person for alleged lies when it is entirely possible that at least one time during their summation or introduction, the defense attorney is going to utter a lie. Or at least a great stretch of the truth to provide a defense for their client.

Misrepresentation

Sometimes, an attorney may try to mention evidence that has previously been disallowed by the judge by asking a witness about it. Alternatively, they may ask a witness for details about something that was excluded from the testimony of a prior witness. This is usually objected to by the opposing attorney, but the damage is done, so to speak, by exposing the jury to that information.

Misrepresentation can also serve as a substitute for hearsay. The hearsay rules were created to guarantee that witness evidence is reliable and credible. The general hearsay rule is that a statement must be made directly to the witness and not repeated to them by a third party.

During witness examination, the attorney may attempt to introduce statements about things that someone has told a witness, but the witness did not actually hear them. This is hearsay and may be quickly challenged; however, the judge may sustain the objection, but the jury has still heard the statement. As a competent juror, you will want to disregard these statements in their entirety.

Also, do not let yourself be confused by the misrepresentation of evidence or witness statements. The defense attorney, during summation, may say something like, "Remember the witness said…" or "Remember the evidence showed by the DNA lab was…" However, if you review the transcripts during deliberation, that may not be true. If it is indeed untrue, that is a big red flag.

In the 2001 murder of Bonny Lee Bakley, the accused, Robert Blake, was seen at the crime scene rubbing his hands on the wet grass. He also said that he returned to the restaurant before reporting his wife as murdered (where he could have washed his hands). The defendant had his hands swabbed for GSR (gunshot residue) with negative results. The defendant's defense attorney said on camera, "You can't wash off GSR completely," but that is not correct. Any competent firearms expert will tell you that gunshot residue can be easily washed away. Statements such as this can certainly mislead a jury.

"You can't wash off GSR completely, so my client didn't shoot a gun."

Defense Witnesses

Defense Expert Witnesses

In many criminal trials, expert witnesses are called to testify and present evidence. Expert witnesses come in all shapes and forms. They can be called for almost any topic that the prosecution wants to present, from technical to scientific.

There appears to be a distinct line between prosecution expert witnesses, who testify about the results of examinations in the course of their employment, and technical/scientific witnesses called to provide their opinions regarding the evidence.

Since court testimony is not a major portion of their job, some prosecution witnesses can be a little shaky and tentative on the stand. Testifying in court is a small percentage of the tasks they do, and sometimes they don't testify for months at a time. For certain job classifications, where the evidence is definitive, they testify less often, as the defendant usually pleads guilty upon learning of the evidence, and the case does not proceed to trial.

In contrast, defense experts are sometimes seasoned courtroom veterans, well used to playing on the jury's susceptibilities. They are accomplished in their court demeanor and performance. These witnesses are selected not only for their testimony but also for their salesmanship. Those who are in most demand are those who can sell not only their conclusions but also their status as experts. They can and should be considered as hired defense witnesses.

An old adage within the legal community is that a jury is often persuaded by the out-of-town witness carrying a suitcase. Do not be swayed because the witness has come from far away to testify or has an extensive résumé. Instead, rely on the evidence presented.

Scientific Witnesses and Hired Defense Witnesses

A scientific witness is called when it is necessary to explain scientifically based evidence, such as fingerprints, DNA, firearms, or electronic or digital forensics. Sometimes a forensic scientist is called to explain the absence of scientific evidence such as why fingerprints are not as common as is generally thought, or what it would mean if there was no foreign DNA recovered at the crime scene.

Generally, witnesses cannot state opinions or give specific conclusions unless they have been deemed experts or specially qualified in that area. Witnesses qualified in a particular field as expert witnesses may provide their opinion based on their knowledge in that field and may also provide the basis for that opinion.

An expert witness or an especially qualified witness will typically be asked voir dire questions to establish their qualifications as experts. In this instance, voir dire questioning involves asking specific questions that elicit their background, knowledge, and experience that qualify them as an expert witness.

Scientific witnesses can also be "hired defense witnesses." As mentioned above, this is a scientific or specialized witness who is paid by the defense to present their testimony. Introducing money interjects automatic bias into the witness's testimony. Sometimes the scientific witness has legitimate information that applies to the case, while at other times it may seem that the presentation is solely intended to provide an alternative theory. These may be more like paid actors who misappropriate science to play upon a juror's emotions.

Sometimes, the hired scientific witness may be well insulated from the day-to-day world of practical forensic analysis, whereas state or government practitioners and scientists conduct day-to-day testing and validation of their analysis of crime scene evidence. These scientists, examiners, and other forensic experts conduct real tests and obtain real results in their regular work experience.

A specialized witness may provide testimony in a field that may or may not be broadly accepted by the general scientific community. This type of testimony may be characterized as *McScience*. McScience is "science" created to support the claims of the defense. This is where the witness presents evidence about a field that may be unusual or not well established.

A historical example of this is the Lindbergh kidnapping and murder trial, where a "wood expert" testified to the wood grain and the wood origin of one piece of the ladder at the Lindbergh residence. This expert even speculated that since the wood piece did not match up and was not the correct size of the wood planks in the defendant's home, it had been altered by a skillful carpenter to become just one of the 17 crosspieces on the poorly made ladder found at the crime scene. Today, this might be considered pseudoscience.

In recent times, a celebrated forensic scientist, Henry Lee, was found liable by a judge for fabricating evidence in a murder case that sent two Connecticut men to prison for decades for a crime they did not commit. Many forensic scientists were skeptical when Henry Lee testified during the O. J. Simpson case about possible footwear impressions, which were primarily based on speculation. During the Simpson trial, Lee also told jurors that there was something wrong with a blood sample placed into evidence, boosting the defense's claim that the police had tampered with the blood evidence.

Superior Qualification Syndrome

Another aspect of technical/scientific witness testimony is the superior qualification syndrome. Superior qualification syndrome occurs when a witness presents an extensive list of qualifications and degrees, as well as numerous instances of court testimony, which can lead the jury to accept their opinion without critical examination. However, these apparently highly qualified witnesses can still be stretching the truth and testifying merely to sow doubt in the minds of the jury, and may not be providing truly beneficial testimony.

Some scientific witnesses, especially those put forth by the defense, may not have the best intentions. Because they are independent and not subject to the typically strict administrative controls of a government agency, they may be overconfident in their ability to form reliable opinions on the scientific aspects of the case.

Alternative Witnesses (WHORES)

A common technique for responding to prosecution witnesses is for the defense to call witnesses that law enforcement has sometimes referred to as a W.H.O.R.E., or a Witness Having Other Reasonless Explanation. This type of witness is introduced to confuse the jury and to dilute any significant evidence a witness may produce. This approach can lead to a witness war that effectively cancels the testimony of witnesses. A juror should be aware of this tactic and understand that a witness may have been scheduled to testify solely for the purpose of influencing the jury.

It may be difficult for the layperson to sort out the sides in a witness war. You will want to evaluate the substance of each person's testimony carefully and not automatically dismiss both witnesses merely because they counter each other. Certain aspects of each witness may have a bearing on the details of the case.

Belief Speaking

Sometimes a witness, usually for the defense, comes across so sincerely that even though they may be stretching the truth, people still believe them. This can be called belief speaking. Belief speaking focuses on the presenter's outward sincerity, often at the expense of factual accuracy. In other words, if the speaker really believes it, that makes it true. Or due to the earnest and heartfelt presentation of the person speaking, what they say is certainly something to consider, no matter how outrageous it is. You should be aware of this phenomenon and not fall for it.

The Untrustworthy Witness

During the trial, several witnesses may take the stand and testify. Some will be called by the prosecution, and some may be called to testify for the defense. The witnesses may contradict each other, and you may have a question about which one is telling the truth.

Everybody thinks they can tell when someone is lying. The truth is, no one can really tell when someone is lying. The age-old techniques, which focus on eye movement, direct eye contact, and, of course, the "lie detector," have been proven, over and over again, to be worthless in detecting a liar. An accomplished liar knows what you are looking for to detect lies. Good liars know to look you in the eye, that they should remain calm, and that they should show confidence in their answers. They can carefully control their nonverbal signals, such as eye movement, facial expressions, hand gestures, and even their breathing.

Some liars are very good at it, and an accomplished liar can easily lie undetected. They trust that they will be believed and think they are smarter than anyone else. Some people lie automatically, even without a real purpose, while others lie to protect themselves.

Good liars are also very skilled at feigning emotions. It can be challenging to determine if they are genuinely emotional due to the incident. They may seem overcome by emotion due to the crime, but are actually putting on an act.

Many of us have experienced a person saying, "So help me God," or "On my mother's life," but we know they are lying.

A little something about liars for you as a juror: accomplished liars aren't worried about manipulating others. They remain confident, forceful, and relaxed as they exploit others. Good liars are essentially great actors. They make a game out of projecting a created, reasonable version of themselves. They play the role of an honest and trustworthy person. They may even rehearse the role and prepare a well-organized tale to seem natural.

As a juror, you need to judge the truthfulness of a witness by the other factors in the case and not by your emotional impressions. In court, a true liar is someone who is shown to be untruthful by other testimony or by the evidence. The lie is verified not by visual cues from the witness but by actual evidence. The lie is uncovered by apparent contradictions through witness testimony and evidence that refutes that person's statements.

An example might be the defendant stating in interviews and through their attorney that they were never at the crime scene, but cell phone tracing shows that their cell phone was there. Or possibly some witnesses saw them there at that time. Or the defendant has stated that they don't own a gun, but the murder weapon was registered to them. Perhaps the defendant said that they never made those computer searches about poisoning, but they were the only one with access to that computer. Or the defendant stated they never handled or touched some important evidence, but their DNA or fingerprints were found on that item. These are all ways that a lie can be determined with evidence, rather than relying on the defendant's or witness's appearance or body language.

Some people who are later found to be liars are viewed as likable, sympathetic, and honest. They can usually fool the people around them, both socially and within their families. The physical evidence of a case should take precedence over any statements made by witnesses or the defendant.

In the documentary *Making a Murderer*, Steven Avery comes across as extremely sincere and appears very believable. However, the vast amount of inculpatory evidence in the case, including some extremely damning evidence not mentioned in the documentary, leads undoubtedly to his guilt in the murder.

The Rotating Story and the Defendant's Lies

The last witness in the trial might be the defendant, and it may be your task to determine if they are telling you the truth from the witness stand or if they told the truth to the police, other people, or other witnesses. If you believe that people are mainly honest and inherently truthful, leave that at the door. People lie. The key is to surmise why they are lying.

It is a truism within the justice system that an innocent person does not change their story because it is the truth. Only a liar, who is making up a story, changes it, either on purpose to make it sound better or inadvertently because they cannot remember their invented tale exactly.

Most detectives believe an innocent person will always tell the same story. There may be small, explainable discrepancies where the person remembers fewer details over time, but the significant details of the incident should remain unchanged if they are truthful. That is why, sometimes, detectives take a cooperating "witness" to the crime scene to re-create the incident. Police are attempting to identify any discrepancies that may occur during the re-creation.

A guilty person changes their story to fit the circumstances, rather than always telling the truth. This will usually be discovered during questioning by the police. An accused person may arrange their story to fit information relayed to them by detectives during questioning. It is typical for interrogating detectives to gradually provide a suspect with more information about the incident to observe how the suspect responds. Frequent alterations of the story, which are adjusted as the police describe time frames, phone calls, video footage, and eyewitness accounts, should lead a juror to consider the possibility that the accused may be lying.

Has the defendant lied during the investigation? Sometimes, it may be revealed in court that the defendant has apparently lied to witnesses and told them varying stories about the crime. Lies by the defendant can be verified by evidence. They weren't in a certain place, didn't know that person, didn't own a gun, or their marriage was perfect with no arguments. All of these things can be verified through witnesses, documents, and physical evidence to determine if the defendant has lied.

Any lie should be given huge consideration by you as a juror. There is a purpose for lies. Lies are typically used to deflect responsibility, blame, and accountability.

It would not be an exaggeration to say that in the Caylee Anthony case, Casey Anthony lied at least fifteen times to investigators. Her lies were easily verified by the police. There was no babysitter named Zanny or Zanita, and no apartment where she lived. Casey even faked a job and the names of her bosses. She gave a few false phone numbers, lied about her car, and lied about what she had been doing for the month before her parents reported her and her daughter missing.

It may help you to decipher the statements made by the defendant to investigators by considering what an innocent person would say or do at that point in the investigation.

A defense attorney may provide an excuse for the evident lies of their client. One such approach that has been offered is that, because the statements were not made under oath in testimony, they couldn't be considered a lie. This, of course, is another bit of defense attorney chicanery.

Look Here - Look Away From There

Beware when the defense begins concentrating on a specific facet of the case or specific evidence in the case to the exclusion of other important evidence. It is usually a distraction designed to focus on one area of evidence while diverting attention away from other important evidence in the case. For example, in the Teresa Halbach murder at Avery's Auto Salvage in Wisconsin, the defense concentrated its attention on blood transfer evidence inside the victim's vehicle. The defense attorney's approach was that specific blood evidence could have been planted, which prompted testimony by an FBI expert to explain how crime scene blood evidence is preserved. This tactic required hours of testimony focused on that specific blood evidence and could have proved to be a distraction from the DNA attributed to the defendant and transferred to other locations within and on the vehicle. The defendant's DNA was found on the area near the battery and inside the vehicle, but the defense had the courtroom focused on the blood evidence.

The defense may state that "there is no [fill in the blank(s)] evidence that supports the allegations submitted by the prosecution." You will want to pay attention to that exact wording.

In the Eric Richins murder case in Summit County, Utah, the prosecution said it had witnesses, family, and friends who could testify that Richins suspected his wife was trying to kill him. The defense attorney stated, "There has not been a single text message or other document... to support the allegation." Any juror should be able to discern the difference between messages, documents, and actual testimony. There may not have been text messages or documents, but there was plenty of other evidence pointing to the killer. The defense was banking on the deflection to text messages and documents to shift the jury away from the actual evidence in the case.

This tactic is designed to discredit certain types of evidence and apply it to other forms of evidence. Don't look there, look here. This is a form of distraction.

Defense Attorney Testifying

If you ever hear a complaint or objection by the opposing counsel that says that the counsel is "testifying," pay attention. This is when the defense begins to interpret the information the witness is providing by repeating it, but with slight changes that either discredit the testimony or subtly alter it to favor their client.

The attorney may also load his questions with his own impressions that can constitute "testifying," such as including in their question information that is not part of the witness's testimony.

This bit of chicanery is usually employed because the lawyer lacks a witness or evidence to counter the witness's testimony on the stand, or the defense attorney wants to confuse the jury.

If it seems that the defense attorney is making up facts you do not remember the witness testifying to, this is when the defense attorney is actually testifying.

Another method of an attorney testifying is when the attorney presents their own personal ideas or opinions as a response to the questions asked. Like "That doesn't seem credible to me," meaning that the witness was lying, or stating, "Well, it seems to me that evidence excludes the defendant, doesn't it?"

Another form of this category is when the attorney laughs noticeably or visibly smirks during witness testimony. This is a calculated operation with several intentional purposes. It can be used to belittle a witness in an attempt to disturb their concentration on the stand, or it can be used to try to influence the jury by providing a personal assessment of the witness's testimony.

Defense Tactics

Theatre

SOMETIMES THE TRIAL BECOMES A THEATRE. THE defense will put on a "play" to present their side of the story. The more dramatic, the more it will leave an impression on the jury. This may entail exaggerated assertions of witness testimony, inflated assessments of police behavior, or overstated accusations about possible other suspects. It may be the attorneys acting out a confrontation in the courtroom to demonstrate how the assault or attack was carried out, or maybe a full-size display of a room recreated in front of the bench. All of this is done for your benefit as a juror. This theatre can help you visualize the crime scene, or it can follow the gaslight deception model, which deflects attention away from the defendant and toward other areas of the case.

Alfred Hitchcock was said to have stated that he could play his audience like a piano, using each "key" to elicit a specific emotional response. It could be said that some defense attorneys, without stating this sentiment out loud, would like to think that they can do this in the courtroom, using these subtle and underhanded tricks to play on your emotions and get you to overlook the facts and evidence in the trial. Some examples of playing to the emotions of a jury might be the audio recordings of Mark Furman in the O.J. trial, or the defense suggesting abuse in the Casey Anthony trial. These elicit such an emotional response that incriminating evidence can take a back seat in the trial.

Emotion

Defense attorneys, facing a tough case with substantial evidence that points toward their client, do not want the case to be about the witnesses and the evidence; they want it to be about emotion. They aim to evoke emotion to sow a seed of doubt in the minds of jurors.

The defense attorney will try to elicit testimony from the witnesses that will tug on your heartstrings or try to provoke your anger about a particular facet of the case. They might try to arouse some emotional concern for the defendant or elicit some anger for the possibility of police incompetence.

"This innocent-looking pillar of the community could never have done that."

Emotion is the lifeblood of a defense attorney's case. The more emotion the defense attorney can evoke, outside the evidence in a case, the better for the defense.

They believe that if they can get a jury emotionally invested in the case, any evidence that points to their client can be neutralized. As a juror, try to remain as objective, impartial, and neutral as possible and not fall for the defense attorney's antics in trying to inject emotion into the case.

Both the defense and the prosecution can use emotion. For example, in the 2004 trial for the murderer of Jeffery Wright in Houston, Texas, even though the autopsy showed he was stabbed 193 times, his wife, Susan, claimed self-defense.

The prosecutor, Kelley Siegler, reenacted the incident by having the blood-stained mattress brought into the courtroom and having a stand-in for the victim tied to the bed frame. The prosecutor straddled the man on top of the mattress and proceeded to pretend to stab the stand-in numerous times, recreating the prosecution's theory of the crime. This demonstration was quite emotional for those in the courtroom that day.

Distractions

The defense case can be all about distractions. One such technique in the courtroom is a deliberate objection intended to disrupt the flow of the opposing side's presentation. The substance of the objection can usually determine this. If it seems unnecessary at the time, it probably is.

An attorney may make multiple objections in an attempt to break the train of thought of the witness and disrupt the flow of the presentation of the opposing attorney. These objections are sometimes successful at flustering the witness.

Similarly, an attorney may intentionally interrupt the witness during their presentation regarding their experience, or if it is a scientific or police witness, their area of expertise.

The attorney may deliberately ruffle papers or even drop a file or book during a witness's testimony in an intentional attempt to distract the jurors. These types of actions may give you a solid clue that the defense attorney realizes the importance of that testimony. Another distraction method is to make verbal remarks or even hand gestures. The attorney may also allow the defendant to do these things because it provides a distraction, but any competent defense counsel would instruct their client to remain still and silent.

The attorney may wheel in a cart loaded with file folders and reference books to give the jury the impression that their side is well prepared, has volumes of evidence to present, and has all the evidence on their side. It is most likely that none of the materials will ever be used, but they serve as a distraction.

A common diversionary tactic is when the defense attorney places a large, tied and wrapped package on the defense table but never opens it. This is a distraction that exploits human curiosity and diverts attention away from the presentation of substantial evidence. It is unsettling for people not to know what is in the package.

One such device often attributed to Clarence Darrow was that of a big cigar with ashes hanging from the end during a trial so that when the cigar was smoked down, the jury's attention would be focused on the long bit of ash, instead of on a damaging witness's testimony. It was said that he put a thin wire in his cigar to control the ashes. As a juror, you should pay attention to these types of courtroom antics and not let them serve as a distraction.

Many types of dirty tricks qualify as distractions. The attorney may, for example, place a display board so that the witness is partially blocked from being seen by some of the people on the jury.

These types of sleight of hand are frequently used to divert your attention while an important witness is testifying, or may be used during the prosecution's summation, especially when they are presenting significant evidence. Be aware of outlandish courtroom antics that can be used to divert your attention from the witness currently on the stand. You should not let distraction or chaos disrupt your normal thought processes when considering the evidence.

Audience Shills

It wouldn't be beyond possible for a defense attorney to place a shill in the audience to try to influence the jury. This poseur's purpose would be to make facial expressions or body movements, enough to get the jury's attention, to try to sway the jury's impression of a witness. In this instance, a charlatan audience member might show a questioning expression while a witness is testifying against the defendant, implying that the witness is not to be believed. Or, conversely, the shill will nod their head in a gesture of agreement while a defense witness is on the stand. There may even be more than one lackey sitting in the courtroom to give the impression that many people agree or disagree with the witness who is testifying. This is a rare but interesting flimflam.

Cult Techniques

Beware of cult initiation techniques. This may sound far-fetched, but for a defense attorney who wants to win the case, and perhaps one who fits the description of a Rambo lawyer, this would not be beyond the realm of possibility.

It seems that the common traits for someone to submit to a cult are praise and adulation, isolation, fear, and joining a group of like-minded people. A skilled attorney could wrap all these traits into a few short paragraphs to try to make the jury fall under their spell, especially if the isolation part is already in place with a sequestered jury. The attorney can praise the jury for their intelligence and perception of the "correct facts" in the case, or state that the jurors are intelligent and perceptive, so they will see through the evidence. Then they might instill a little fear in the jury by implying that if they don't conclude in a certain way, they may be looked upon with scorn by the public, trying to make the jury feel that their decision can affect their lives. This tactic takes attention away from the defendant, but even more, it personalizes the case in terms of how it affects the jury, their conscience, and their morality. Then the attorney might assume that the entire jury shares the same mindset regarding their appraisal of the evidence.

It is possible that the defense attorney may incorporate several of these cult techniques when speaking to the jury during summation.

Offered Defenses

SEDI & SOS

Quite often, a defense proffered in court is either the SEDI or the SOS defense. "The defendant didn't do it, Someone Else Did It" (SEDI), or "Some Other Sucker did it" (SOS).

The defense attorney using SOS is not pursuing justice or seeking to solve the case; they want to point the finger at someone else and create doubt in the minds of the jury. They are trying to get you to think, "Well, maybe, just maybe, it could have been someone else."

In some cases, the attorney will present an alternative suspect, usually without a great deal of substance, blaming someone else who may have a motive—a family member, a friend, or an ex-spouse—but it is most likely someone who has already been vetted by the prosecution and eliminated as a suspect.

The SEDI may also be someone anonymous. Someone

unknown could have had access to the crime scene or possibly committed the crime.

Another version of this nefarious deflection is TODDI, "This Other Dude Did It." The intent remains the same: to point to someone else in order to muddy the circumstances of the case.

This can seem like an effective defense, especially if a TODDI suspect might have a possible motive, an unproven alibi, or some other suspicious behavior from which the defense could weave an alternate story, perhaps even despite the evidence.

You may hear the defense counsel point to someone else who had the "motive, means, and opportunity to commit the crime," but consider all the other details, such as the guilty conduct before and after the crime, that allowed the prosecution to focus on just one individual, the defendant. Also, consider the circumstantial factors of the case that may directly lead to the defendant.

In the 2019 murder of Maria Cuevas-Garcia, a 58-year-old Pueblo, Colorado, mother, her dismembered body was found both in a car wash's dumpster and in a trash bag beside the Arkansas River. The defense in the case listed several actions that the defendant took that "he regrets," including the disposal of his mother's dismembered torso, theft from her pickup truck, and using a check stolen from the truck to withdraw $250, in addition to fleeing from police. However, the defense maintained that the defendant did not kill his mother. Instead, the defense attorney alluded to "bad blood" between another woman and the victim, including that each woman believed the other was a "witch." An example of SEDI in action.

Interestingly, in the Cuevas-Garcia case, the prosecution said DNA was found inside a pair of rubber gloves located in the area where Cuevas-Garcia's body was likely dismembered, and where the defendant was seen on surveillance video dumping a suitcase containing the dismembered body of his mother. Additionally, a recorded confession from the defendant was obtained.

If the defense gives you another trail to go down, seeking an alternate suspect, consider this avenue very carefully. Is it merely a rabbit hole to confuse you and detract from the substance of the case? The other suspect may have had a motive (everyone hated the victim), the means (a violent past), and even the opportunity (their alibi is not rock solid), but it is your task as a juror to weigh the circumstances and decide if they counterbalance all of the details presented about the defendant. Is the alternate scenario legitimate or a diversion?

The SEDI defense appeared prominently in Bonnie Lee Bakley Blake's murder trial in Los Angeles in 2004. The defense suggested that Bakley's provocative past may have led to her murder to try to counter the prosecution's evidence that included two former stuntmen saying Robert Blake tried to hire them to kill his wife (and used a clandestine calling card to contact them), that he was at the scene of the crime, that an antique gun, similar to one Blake's assistant possessed, was found feet from the scene, that there was testimony about numerous murder plots, and there was a suspicious list written by his assistant that included "two shovels, small sledge, crowbar, 25 auto, get blank gun ready, old rags, duct tape, pool acid, and lye."

If the defense presents one or more suspects with little or weak evidence as being the real culprits, look at this with great suspicion. If the defense truly had reason to believe that someone else was responsible, they would likely have hired their own detectives to pursue those leads. If they could develop leads and have some viable proof, they would have certainly presented this to the police, and the trial wouldn't even be happening.

In perhaps one of the ultimate SEDI cases, some other *dudes* did do it. The defendant, accused of killing his 77-year-old mother, Shirley Meritt, said two armed men came into his home and stabbed his mother in front of him. The defendant, a disbarred lawyer, told the Georgia court that this happened on the very day he was supposed to turn himself in after he was convicted of stealing more than half a million dollars from seventeen former clients in Cobb County. He said that even though he was not harmed, he was so scared, he cut off his ankle monitor, changed his name and appearance, ran away, and was in hiding until he was finally arrested by U.S. Marshals a state away in Tennessee.

Remember that when the defense presents an SOS defense, separately isolate all the evidence pointing at the defendant and then attempt to apply it to the SOS suspect. Usually, because the prosecution and defense have already conducted this exercise repeatedly while preparing the case, the evidence will be very weak when applied to the SEDI suspect.

This "someone else did it" became a part of a famous

California case in the late 1940s when Caryl Chessman, known as the Red Light Bandit, was convicted of a large number of assault and robbery crimes. Chessman was on San Quentin's death row for 12 years and was eventually executed. He wrote several books while in prison, defended himself in court, and suggested he knew who the real Bandit was, but refused to reveal the information.

A juror should not allow this tactic of a "real suspect" to sway their thinking about the evidence. A juror should concentrate on the evidence being presented and not be distracted by the implication by the defense that some unknown person could be the real guilty party.

Take the evidence and link it to the person they are claiming could have committed the crime. What person could have left that evidence? What person had the means, motive, opportunity, *and* guilty conduct before and after the crime? Usually, only one person could fit all of those categories.

Blame the Victim

In keeping with the "hammer" concept, a defense attorney may use victim blaming as a platform during their defense. These cases can involve an attack on the victim's reputation. The defense may present witnesses to testify that the victim had a dubious reputation, or the defense may elicit testimony from prosecution witnesses regarding the victim's questionable character. The implication, almost always unspoken, is that the victim perhaps drew their own fate or deserved what they got.

In the 2019 Andreen McDonald murder case in San

Antonio, Texas, the defendant was seen on video purchasing an axe, a log-splitter, and several heavy-duty trash bags. In the trial, the defendant admitted to disposing of and burning his wife's body and burning her clothes. However, the defense implied, and the defendant implied in his testimony, that the victim was at fault and that she had caused the entire incident through her actions, such as hiding financial transactions from him.

In another case from 2019, before the defendant's suicide (in which according to police, he was seen dumping bags and other items at 30 different locations, including trash cans and in a storm drain), the defense for the Connecticut man charged in the Jennifer Dulos murder case stated that they believed the victim had caused her own disappearance in a plot to receive medical treatment. The defense also suggested that she staged her disappearance to resolve issues in the contentious divorce proceedings.

No matter how shoddy, disreputable, controversial, or scurrilous the reputation of the victim is, it is your responsibility to decide if the evidence of the crime still points to the defendant.

The Devil Made Me Do It

From a mere excuse for horrible behavior to the suggestion that the devil actually possessed the defendant, "The devil made me do it" has been used as the defense in a range of crimes.

In a 1981 murder trial that took place in Connecticut, the defendant, Arne Cheyenne Johnson, attempted to place blame for his killing of Alan Bono on possession by the devil. Johnson denied committing the crime, despite eyewitness testimony. The defendant eventually switched his argument from possession to self-defense and was only convicted of manslaughter.

In a 2017 case in San Antonio, Texas, a man was arrested on a charge of indecent sexual contact with a child and reportedly blamed his behavior on the devil's influence. The child's mother offered to rid the defendant of the devil. However, the defendant stated that the devil had already left. The defendant was found guilty in 2018.

In Texas in 2016, a 20-year-old told the police that he shot two 13-year-old girls after talking with the devil. He was convicted of murder.

Fortunately, these defenses rarely succeed in getting the defendants acquitted.

Police Malfeasance

The defense counsel in your case may propose that the police botched the investigation. A juror needs to realize that even the most botched crime scene can still reveal the true perpetrator of the crime. A mismanaged crime scene does not automatically mean that the defendant is innocent.

Although it is very rare for police to botch an investigation completely, it is common for law enforcement to make mistakes. They may mishandle evidence, they may conduct incomplete interviews, and they may make errors in their reports. However, these problems in the investigation, even if all of the above do occur, do not automatically mean that all the evidence can be dismissed. It does not mean that the entire case against the defendant should be rejected due to police malfeasance.

Even if the crime scene was compromised, it does not necessarily indicate the defendant's innocence. In the Nicole Brown and Ronald Goldman murder case, some procedures were surely botched, and evidence may have been mishandled. However, this case was one that had the most incriminating evidence in all of the history of criminal justice.

Inadequate documentation or insufficient evidence collection does not mean the entire case was compromised. If the defense claims that a flawed investigation led to the collection of inadequate evidence, which could have implicated the "real suspect," this does not necessarily mean that the collected evidence is tainted.

Indeed, if the police make a mistake in one facet of the investigation, it should not follow that all the evidence should be disregarded. One issue should not be elongated to include all the evidence in a case. Even multiple mistakes should not mean that every facet of the prosecution's case should be dismissed.

Defense attorneys have presented witnesses who specialize in police procedure to question the methods employed in a police investigation. They may be able to demonstrate how a particular investigation deviated from generally accepted law enforcement practices or even how the police failed to follow their own policies. This testimony should not necessarily void the evidence recovered and should not cancel out the other evidence in the case.

The inference that something was not processed for fingerprints or DNA should not be given unwarranted weight. Missed or destroyed evidence is only relevant if it disputes the other facts in the case.

If it is indeed proven by testimony that mistakes were made, this may not hold true for the entire police investigation. A juror should not fall for the implication that, because the investigation was shoddy, the defendant is innocent.

The defense attorney may also suggest that had the crime scene or the investigation not been so compromised, another suspect or "the real suspect" could have been identified. This approach has the same logic as the SEDI approach. One does not automatically follow the other, nor does it make sense. The investigators might not have followed up on a lead, or they might not have recovered an item of possible evidence, but it is illogical to suggest that the real suspect would have been uncovered. Would anyone else fit all of the circumstances present that point to the defendant? Consider the entirety of the case before falling into the trap that someone else could have been the real culprit.

"The police so botched this case, you must acquit the defendant."

Rush to Judgment

While there have been cases where a police investigation rushed to judgment, it does not automatically make the person at the center of the investigation innocent. A rush to judgment occurs when police or law enforcement have already formed a conclusion before initiating their investigation. The assumption is that the police dismiss all other lines of inquiry to concentrate solely on one person.

Similar to the claim of police malfeasance, the rush to judgment theory raises concerns about the credibility of investigating officers, potentially allowing the real criminal to go undetected. A key part of this theory is that investigators fail to gather crucial evidence or information, thereby casting doubt on the case itself. The rush to judgment theory is a common attempt to discredit the police investigation in a case. The implication is that, due to a rush to judgment, the police arrested the wrong person, and the "real suspect" is still at large.

In the O.J. Simpson trial, an outside scientific witness testified that the police did not collect a possible footwear impression that was photographed on the walkway, implying that the footprint could have been that of the real suspect. Other witnesses testified that the photograph actually depicted a disruption in the construction of the walkway and was not a footwear impression at all.

The defense may also use the term tunnel vision. Tunnel vision is another name for the rush to judgment defense, implying that the prosecution focused only on the defendant from the early stages of the investigation.

In the 2022 Anna Wilson murder case, the prosecution presented digital evidence against the defendant, a romantic rival of the victim, including a video placing the defendant's vehicle at the scene, as well as DNA evidence from a discarded bike near the victim's apartment. The defense argued that the prosecution had tunnel vision in the case, focusing solely on the defendant and failing to consider other potential suspects. The defense wanted the jury to dismiss all that evidence due to tunnel vision by the prosecution.

Dovetailed with the rush to judgment, the accusation may be an attack on the prosecutor's motivation, implying that the indictment, investigation, or prosecution is biased against the defendant. This may have a political or financial orientation.

A juror should carefully weigh the significance of this claim. Even if there is a significant presumption of a preexisting bias toward a specific person, it does not dismiss the cumulative evidence in the case. If the investigation still uncovered substantial evidence pointing to the defendant, then the potential bias should not be allowed to discount that evidence. The charge of tunnel vision by the police or some form of hyperfocus or bias is not a valid reason for excluding all the evidence.

"I Panicked."

There have been cases where a defense attorney has presented the "I panicked" justification as a defense. The victim was already dead, killed by either someone else or died by natural means, and "I panicked." The "I panicked and had to get rid of the body but didn't kill them" excuse should be met with intense suspicion by jurors.

Astonishingly, the "I panicked" defense has been presented many times and is usually designed to deflect from the cause of death.

In a 1973 case in Maine, Richard Rogers was on trial for the murder of Frederic Spencer. Roger's attorney presented a defense that Rogers killed Spencer by hitting him multiple times with a hammer in self-defense, then he panicked and smothered the victim with a plastic bag, wrapped him up in a plastic tent, and disposed of the body along a road, miles from Rogers' home.

If there is ever a statement that the defendant panicked or was distressed, which accounts for their unusual behavior, it can be added to the assessment of the overall evidence; however, it should be combined with all the other evidence. For example, suppose other unusual behavior occurred, such as not calling the police right away. In that case, that behavior can be considered, but if there is a pattern of unusual behavior similar to this, if the defendant then moved the body and told friends or a lawyer before calling the police, this all can be given additional weight.

The Defendant In-Court Outburst

In a gimmicky, dirty trick that may or may not be sanctioned by the defense attorney, the defendant may make certain verbal or physical outbursts in the courtroom.

In the Avante Boyce murder trial in San Antonio in 2023, the defendant had an emotional outburst and had to be escorted out of the courtroom. The question was, "Did he do that to intimidate the jury?"

Murder For Hire

In cases where a hitman was involved, the defense may claim the hitman took it upon themself to do the murder. It is certainly a stretch of credulity to believe that a hitman decided on their own to commit a murder.

In the 2014 murder case of Dan Markel in Florida, it was determined that the defendant hired a set of hitmen to commit the murder. The defendant's defense in the Markel case was that the hitmen murdered the victim essentially "on spec," with the anticipation that the defendant's family would pay them, then extorted the defendant for money. Of course, a juror should have difficulty accepting this scenario.

The Incompetent Attorney Defense

Maybe one of the most insidious defense attorney dirty tricks is the incompetent attorney defense. This chicanery occurs when the defense is purposely so bad in defending their client that they are setting things up for an easy appeal based upon the quality of counsel. This type of defense typically occurs when the client is so difficult to represent that they are stubborn or defiant and do not listen to their attorney. This type of client may make comments at press conferences or on social media that seem to undermine the defense and may even inadvertently incriminate themselves. The defense attorney seems to have no choice but to do such a bad job, usually in cleverly subtle ways, to establish a platform for future appeals.

A retrial on appeal usually favors the defendant, as witnesses' memories fade and people are unavailable or even die before a retrial comes to court. An advantage of the incompetent attorney defense is that a case that wins on appeal and must be retried will be more difficult for the prosecution to prove.

Thankfully, this type of defense is very rare.

Additional Extraordinary Defenses

Self Defense

One widespread defense offered is self-defense. This is where a person was afraid for their own well-being and took action to protect themselves from harm. In these cases, a juror should look for the defense attorney to fully demonstrate that the defendant was in imminent danger and in fear for their life.

Self-defense is usually defined as using reasonable force to protect someone from immediate harm. The force must match the threat faced, and the belief in the danger must be reasonable.

In these types of cases, it can be difficult for a juror to distinguish between overt reckless retaliation and legitimate use of force for protection.

Sometimes, a victim or defendant will plead self-defense, but it is later determined, through testimony, that it was not self-defense at all.

One such case occurred in Minnesota in 2012, where

Byron Smith killed two burglars inside his home and pleaded self-defense. Smith said the burglars, a young man and a young woman, had weapons and were threatening his life, so he shot them. Smith forgot that he had an audio tape running that recorded his actions and revealed that he was not under threat. After the investigation, it was determined that Smith had set up his home to catch and kill the burglars.

In the murders of Saiveon Pugh and Jessie Ransom in Columbus, Georgia, the defense proposed that the fifty gunshots that were directed at the victims were done in self-defense. The prosecutor stated they had eyewitnesses and video of the incident showing how the defendants lay in wait for the victims. Self-defense did not seem appropriate in that case.

A jury should consider all the pertinent background when self-defense is presented during a trial. Was there past experience with threats of injury? Was the victim physically intimidating? Was there a history of confrontation between the defendant and the victim? Did the defendant believe their life was in danger, and could the danger have reasonably been carried out?

In a 2024 trial in New Hampshire for the murder and dismemberment of the body of Emily Jean Schwarz-Ferlazzo in 2021, though the defendant, her husband, claimed self-defense, the defense was unable to provide any significant background support. During Emily Ferlazzo's autopsy, the medical examiner noted that she was about 5'3" and weighed about 128 pounds, and that she had 16 stab wounds to her upper body and was shot twice in the head. During the trial, the defendant testified that his wife had punched and kicked him before the shooting; however, crime scene photos showed no injuries to the defendant.

"That is not a confession; he was merely writing a murder mystery novel."

Insanity Defense

The insanity defense can be the most difficult defense for a juror to consider. An insanity plea by a defendant in a trial poses several challenging issues for a jury.

An insanity plea is based upon the presentation that the defendant usually admits culpability (they did it), but is pleading not guilty by reason of insanity. The claim is that the defendant was so mentally impaired as to not know right from wrong or not be capable of making a mental decision that the act was illegal or immoral.

There will usually be psychiatrists presenting testimony in favor of the defendant and those called by the prosecution to oppose the defense. They will present testimony to determine whether the defendant is competent or incompetent to stand trial for the offense.

Sometimes it seems as if the psychiatrists in an insanity plea trial may fit the "hired defense witness" category or the "witness having another reasonless explanation" category. It can undoubtedly be difficult for a juror to discern if "belief speaking" or "superior qualification syndrome" is coming into play with the psychiatrist(s) providing testimony.

An interesting insanity plea trial occurred during a

2012 trial in Georgia, during which some "devil made me do it" type presentations were produced. A defendant was on trial for the 2010 murder of Russell Sneiderman outside of a Dunwoody daycare center. Evidence was presented that the defendant, possibly wearing a black fake beard, had rented the car seen on video at the crime scene and that the defendant had a relationship with the victim's wife. Evidence was also presented that the gun used was linked to the defendant's wife, and black synthetic fibers, such as those used in a fake beard, were found in the rented vehicle.

During the trial, the defense represented that the defendant was visited by a demon that had the voice of Barry White and by an angel that sounded like Olivia Newton-John, who told him the victim needed to die.

The defendant was found guilty but mentally ill; however, the Georgia Supreme Court reversed the conviction in favor of the defendant. The defendant was then found guilty of Russell Sneiderman's murder in a subsequent trial in 2016.

Twinkie Defense

During the Dan White trial in 1979, the term "Twinkie Defense" was created in the press after White's lawyer claimed that before the crime, White had been diagnosed with depression, which made him crave sweets such as Twinkies. White was accused of killing San Francisco Mayor George Moscone and Supervisor Harvey Milk. White, a former city supervisor, snuck into the city building and shot the men in their offices. White's lawyer claimed it was the depression that led him to commit the murder. Astonishingly, the jury only convicted White of manslaughter.

Sleepwalking Defense

A defense psychiatrist testified in the 1982 trial of Steven Steinberg that Steinberg had no "logical, rational motive" to kill his wife and was probably sleepwalking when he stabbed her twenty-six times with a kitchen knife.

Steinberg admitted in court to killing his wife but claimed that it happened while he was sleepwalking. His lawyer entered a temporary insanity plea, and Steinberg was found not guilty. Startlingly, since it was only temporary insanity, Steinberg was set free, despite the murder.

In another sleepwalking case that occurred in 2017, Brooke Preston was stabbed by her roommate, who claimed he was sleepwalking at the time of the crime. At the trial, another roommate (Preston's sister) said that she had never seen the defendant sleepwalking. The defendant in this case was found guilty.

Affluenza Defense

The affluenza defense means that the defendant is too affluent to have committed the crime, or more specifically, that their wealth prevented them from understanding the consequences of their actions. After being caught on surveillance video stealing two cases of beer from a Walmart in Texas, 16-year-old Ethan Couch, driving his father's truck on a restricted license, was speeding at 70 mph and crashed into a crowd, killing four people and injuring nine. Couch had a blood alcohol content of three times the legal limit and also tested positive for marijuana and Diazepam.

At the 2013 trial, Couch's lawyer presented a defense that he couldn't be held accountable because his parents never taught him that evil deeds have consequences. A defense psychologist testified that the teen was a product of "affluenza," a name attributed to a possible mental condition in which a person does not have the capacity to link their actions with consequences because their parents did not teach him that life skill and because their parents' wealth showed them only privilege. In this case, amazingly, the judge merely sentenced the teenager to probation and time in a rehabilitation facility.

The Spray Tan Defense

In the 2012 trial for the murder of Eleonora "Lina" Kaufman, the initial defense was that the victim died as a result of a pre-existing heart condition aggravated by a spray tan. The defense maintained throughout the trial that the husband was innocent, arguing that his wife died from a pre-existing heart condition. Surprisingly, the defendant was acquitted in the case.

The Weak Link Juror

Be fully aware that ***you*** *may be the target of the defense attorney. One tactic for the defense is to find someone in the jury box whom they can dupe or deceive into finding reasonable doubt, using all the tricks of the trade as enumerated in this book.*

You don't want to be the weak link juror. The defense, along with the jury consultants they hire, will be looking for a weak link among the jurors. A person they can overwhelm, a person they can gaslight and confuse, so that the juror cannot make an informed decision and will end up leaning toward acquitting the defendant.

Defense attorneys may hire consultants specifically to identify potential jurors they can target. They will specifically use language during the questioning of witnesses that may be designed to fit the jury consultant's profile of a weak link juror. The attorney may use questioning that is more emotional, more direct, or even call witnesses whom they think the target will relate to. Recognize that the defense may be using this dirty trick, trying to find the weak link juror. Don't let it be you.

Closing Arguments

After both the prosecution and the defense finish their presentations of their case, the next thing that happens in the courtroom is the summation or closing arguments. The purpose of closing arguments is to promote and enhance the jury's proper analysis of the evidence so that it may arrive at a just and fair-minded conclusion based solely on the evidence presented in the trial.

The prosecution attorney usually goes first in closing arguments, but this can vary across different jurisdictions. The lawyer summarizes and comments on the evidence in the most favorable light for their side, highlighting how it supports their assumptions in the case.

After the prosecution has made its case, the defense then presents its closing arguments. The defense lawyer will typically respond to statements made in the prosecution's closing arguments. They will attempt to highlight the issues with the prosecution's case and then summarize the facts favorable to their client.

The defense will almost always propose that the state, also known as the prosecution, has failed to prove its case beyond a reasonable doubt. This will happen in almost every trial. You should not be surprised to hear this. However, this is the opinion of the defense attorney, and you should make your decision on the evidence, not opinions.

A sneaky trick used by defense attorneys is to add their personal opinions into their summation. They may say things like a witness lied during their testimony, without anything having been substantiated. Or they may characterize specific scientific evidence slightly differently than was presented during testimony to try to minimize its impact.

Another instance of mendacity occurs when, during summation, the defense attorney misstates the law. This can occur when the defense attorney discusses the burden of proof and attempts to redefine it beyond a reasonable doubt. The defense attorney may say that the proper definition is that it's beyond all doubt, or that "if you have a doubt, then you have to acquit." These statements are misrepresentations of the law and are designed to influence you as a juror.

Since this is the end of the trial, you will have to sift through the lawyer's final statements and determine which arguments, affirmations, comments, and declarations you believe properly characterize the facts presented.

Reasonable Doubt

The issue of reasonable doubt will surely be mentioned during summations. It is essential to understand that just *any* doubt is not enough to be a reasonable doubt. No case will be entirely without doubt or without any unanswered questions. That is the nature of crime.

A juror should not fall prey to the reasonable doubt myth, that any doubt is the same as reasonable doubt. When confronted with substantial cumulative evidence, you should be careful not to let some doubt serve as a rationalization to vote not guilty. It is a very human emotion to have some doubt; it is normal, but a decision should be based solely on a purely objective, detached review of the evidence.

The predominant formula for defense attorneys in a criminal trial is to try to cast doubt, "reasonable doubt," on the prosecution's case. This is also a prime place where deceitful defense attorneys employ underhanded tactics.

Reasonable doubt can come from a solid alibi. It can be eyewitness testimony from a single witness. It can be opposing eyewitnesses. An irrational timeline can give you reasonable doubt. But reasonable doubt should not automatically be any of the many typical defenses proffered by defense attorneys, like SEDI, police malfeasance, rush to judgment, contamination, or the many other strategies and tactics highlighted in this book. Also, reasonable doubt is not automatically mandated in a "circumstantial" case.

Keep in mind that when the primary defense is that there is obviously reasonable doubt, it is usually not that the defendant is provably innocent; rather, the defense is insisting that the prosecution has not proven the case beyond a reasonable doubt. Remember, when contemplating and evaluating reasonable doubt, this concept is not about social justice, but rather about whether the evidence, for the most part, suggests that the defendant is likely to have committed the crime.

A typical strategy might involve attempting to find enough anomalies in the story presented by the prosecution, no matter how trivial or minuscule, to raise some doubt. They may point out some peculiarities and deviations, which there almost always are in a criminal case, and they may hope some doubts creep in. Throw in the allusion to police mismanagement or misconduct, and this is the formula for creating doubt in a case. As a juror, you can prevent this subterfuge from seizing your thinking by understanding the true meaning of reasonable doubt.

In a criminal trial, the burden of proof rests with the prosecution to prove beyond a reasonable doubt that the defendant is guilty. This means that the defendant does not need to prove their innocence; they only need to raise a reasonable doubt. The burden of proof, in this context, should be considered achievable through normal means. It should not be placed in some unattainable category that is impossible to obtain. The question is: Has the prosecution provided enough points of evidence to make their case that the defendant is the one who committed the crime?

If the prosecution has satisfied the burden of proof, it follows that the case has been presented to a point beyond a reasonable doubt. Remember, reasonable doubt is not mere possible doubt, because everything relating to human affairs is open to some possible doubt.

Reasonable doubt is beyond mere suspicion and is supported by circumstantial evidence that surpasses that doubt. Obtaining the condition of beyond a reasonable doubt is a balancing act. Beyond a reasonable doubt is answered by answering the following question: Do the mitigating circumstances of the defendant outweigh the mitigating factors that are unanswered or that point away from the defendant? Mitigation is the act of alleviating, lessening, or weakening. Do the positive aspects of the defendant's defense, which lessen culpability, outweigh the factors that point to their guilt?

Consider this. Reasonable doubt is the doubt that a reasonable person, like you, might have when considering all the evidence in the case. Not the complete absence of any doubt. Not without *any* question at all, but a realistic, rational interpretation of the evidence. Due to the random, unpredictable nature of crime, not every part of the evidence must be explained or qualified to reach the point of beyond a reasonable doubt.

You do not "have to put the gun in his hands" (or any weapon) to convict someone. When you don't have an eyewitness, which is in almost every case, you will not have that kind of direct evidence. However, you can figuratively put the "gun in his hands" by the accumulation of evidence.

Motive

Motive is often a crucial element in summations. Motive is a very elusive concept, and a juror should not be consumed by trying to determine the motive of the crime. Presenting the motive in a criminal case is not a requirement; it is not an element of proving a crime. It can be a convincing factor in the case, providing a plausible reason why the person committed the crime, but it is not essential to reach a conclusion.

The prosecution may present a possible motive, drawing from some of the common ones such as hate, finances, jealousy, revenge, and mental illness. It is normal for humans to consider why someone would commit a crime, but motive shouldn't be a burden on the juror in making a decision in a criminal case.

You should not confuse motive with intent. The person *intended* to accomplish a goal when committing the crime. Motive, while it is a human element in explaining why someone commits a crime, is not required in most jurisdictions to prove that a crime was committed.

In a 2015 murder case in Virginia, the defense attorney pressed an approach that questioned any motive of the defendant; therefore, the prosecution could not say how the murder was committed or why. In that case, the overdose death of AJ Hadsell, the defendant, the victim's stepfather, had heroin, the weapon of death, in his residence, and had recently bought heroin from his drug dealer. The defendant had also broken into another residence and placed the victim's jacket there to implicate a friend of the victim. The defendant's vehicle was seen near the victim's residence on the day of her disappearance, and the GPS on his van, tracked on the day of the disappearance, led police directly to the victim's body at an abandoned house. Though a motive in the case was never established, the trial judge noted that the evidence against the defendant was "overwhelming."

Various Versions of the Incident

During summations, you will possibly hear various versions of the crime from the attorneys. Remember that the defense, as part of the discovery process, has had access to all the reports, evidence, and witness statements for months, sometimes years, to plan their defense. They have been able to prepare a defense to refute the evidence, but they have also crafted a narrative that aligns with the evidence. It is the job of a defense attorney to counter the evidence presented by the prosecution.

Some responses should be looked upon with great skepticism. Don't automatically buy the story that the wife left her two kids, her phone, and her purse at the house and just ran away. Look upon the scenario given by the defense that the defendant buried his wife in the woods after she accidentally died or died of natural causes with wariness. Be pragmatic when the defense suggests that the victim was already dead when they got there.

Another scenario or version of the incident might be that the victim's death was an accident, even though the defendant had initiated the action that led to their death. The defendant says that they did hit the victim, or swung the bat or the hammer, but never intended to cause death. The objective was merely to harm the victim, not cause their death. Or maybe they did bring a gun to the meeting, but they claim it accidentally went off, that they never intended to actually use the gun to shoot the victim. Alternate versions of the crime, like these, can be very subtle and must be supplemented with the additional circumstances of the case to discern the truth.

In the 2020 murder of Maria Muñoz, in Laredo, Texas, the defense was that the defendant, a medical doctor, had injected his wife with drugs, not to kill her, but to calm her down to discuss their divorce. The defendant did not intend to kill his wife; it was an accident, even though he committed the act that eventually killed her.

"I panicked; that is why I had to dismember the body and put it in all those dumpsters."

Premeditated

Another concept typically presented during summations is premeditation. This can be a confusing concept for jurors. In most jurisdictions, murder and attempted murder are categorized, by definition, into premeditated vs. intentional but unplanned. These are sometimes referred to as first-degree and second-degree.

First-degree or premeditated is generally defined as an act that requires consideration and deliberation. This means that the person planned the act, thought it through, and then carried it out, sometimes prearranging a weapon or other circumstances. It was conceived, plotted, coordinated, and carried out.

Second-degree, or intentional but unplanned, is usually defined as an act that was intentional but not planned before the crime. This may be where a person acts in the heat of the moment. It is an unplanned or impulsive act.

One of the confusing components of premeditation is the time frame. In most jurisdictions, the time frame alone does not determine a premeditated action. Of course, if a significant time frame exists, that is a major factor. If the act was planned well in advance, it makes it easier to determine premeditation.

Unfortunately, no specific formula exists for determining whether a defendant deliberated before committing an act. Was there evidence of any preplanning, such as texts or notes showing intent? Receipts of items purchased to assist in the crime? Overt actions, such as traveling to the scene for a confrontation? Was there a period of time when the defendant could have stopped the act but chose not to, instead thinking about it and continuing anyway? An incident where some neighbors are feuding, and after a verbal confrontation, one man pulls out a gun, and as the other runs away he is shot in the back.

Premeditation in most states only requires that the defendant ponders and considers the act, regardless of the amount of time involved. It can be that the defendant grabs a handy weapon and uses it to kill. People can premeditate and deliberate in a matter of minutes, or even seconds. As a juror, you might be charged with determining premeditation based on all the evidence presented.

A defendant in the 2015 Mary Yoder poisoning murder case was charged with premeditated murder. The prosecutors were able to trace a letter blaming the victim's son and detailing the location of a poison bottle and purchase receipt in his vehicle to the defendant due to her DNA on the bottle. The use of prepaid cards bought by the defendant confirmed the purchase of the poison by the defendant. A computer search by the defendant listed the poison and the fatal amount. The defendant worked for the victim and had a relationship with the son. The defendant stated in interviews that the reason the victim's son would kill his mother was for the inheritance, in an attempt to deflect attention from herself. All of these things showed apparent premeditation on her part. However, the trial resulted in a hung jury. It appears that the jurors were unable to agree on the issue of premeditation.

Malice Aforethought and Intent

A concept that is mentioned along with premeditation is malice aforethought. The typical definition of malice aforethought is that the killer had the intention, or design and purpose, to kill or harm the victim. This is a separate concept from premeditated, and means that the defendant did not plan the killing but did in fact cause the death. In legal situations, intent is a specific mental state that involves a conscious decision to commit the act, whereas malice is a more general concept encompassing various forms of wrongful intent to cause harm. For example, malice aforethought may occur in a death that happened while a person was committing another felony, such as burglary or robbery.

In general terms, a killing qualifies as murder in the first degree when it is committed with premeditation, malice aforethought, and deliberation. Malice aforethought typically involves deliberation and premeditation. Though all three are not required, they usually occur together. Heat of passion would not typically qualify as a defense. The judge can help you with these definitions.

The defense presented in court during the 1989 trial for the murder of actress Rebecca Schaeffer was that it was an impulsive act without premeditation. The Los Angeles prosecutor, Marsha Clark, showed the defendant's video interview where he stated that he was on a "mission" and highlighted his personality as a compulsive planner, a history of stalking celebrities, and an interest in previous celebrity murders. Marsha Clark also revealed how he traveled from Tucson carrying a .357 revolver with him and a copy of the book *The Catcher in the Rye*. This was the book Mark David Chapman had with him when he murdered John Lennon. The defendant was convicted of first-degree, aggravated murder.

"Yes, the defendant caused death but did not have malice aforethought."

After the Trial

Judge's Instructions

THE JUDGE WILL PROVIDE JURORS WITH instructions at various points during the trial about certain aspects of the case—subtleties, complexities, and technicalities—that have been introduced during the trial. Your judge will instruct you on the relevant laws that should guide your jury deliberations. The judge may also elect to discuss specific issues in the case and define any terms or words that may not be familiar to the jurors.

A trial judge will typically explain the standard of proof that jurors should apply to the case, including the application of the "beyond a reasonable doubt" standard in a criminal case. The judge may also advise the jury that you are the sole determiner of the facts and the credibility (believability) of witnesses.

Jury instructions from the judge provide guidance on how the jury should address the legal issues in the case and the substance of the relevant law. They can also be instructions on how to keep on track during deliberations and how to reach a verdict.

In some cases, the judge may instruct the jurors to base their conclusions solely on the evidence presented during the trial, and that the opening and closing arguments of the lawyers are not evidence, but rather the attorneys' statements.

Often, jury instructions are prepared in writing by the judge and read aloud to the jury to inform them on how to act when deciding a case. Jury instructions can provide a kind of flowchart indicating what verdict jurors should achieve based on what they determine to be true before declaring the defendant guilty or not guilty.

Jury Deliberations

After hearing the final arguments and receiving the judge's jury instructions, the jury retires to the jury room to begin deliberating. This is when that evidence tower you have been building comes into play. You have probably created your own building of evidence, perhaps brick by brick, to complete your perception of what happened in this crime, as close to the truth as possible. Keep an open mind because other jurors may be able to contribute to your tower or show some cracks in the works. This is what jury deliberations are all about.

Jury deliberations are when the members of the jury discuss and debate the evidence of the case. Jury members are typically not allowed to access any outside information on the case and should not consider any evidence that was not presented in the trial.

It is customary in most states that the first order of business in jury deliberations is to elect one of the jurors as the foreperson. This elected person's role is to preside over discussions and votes of the jurors, and can be the person who reads the jury's verdict to the court.

You may notice that a bailiff, or court officer, is constantly on hand to ensure that no one communicates with the jury during deliberations. The bailiff will also be available to relay any communications you may need to have with the judge. You or other jurors may have a question about the evidence or the judge's instructions. You may then give a note to the bailiff to take to the judge. The judge may respond to the note or may call the jury back into the courtroom for clarification.

In some jurisdictions, the jury may view and discuss the physical exhibits introduced into the record in the jury room. The jury can also request that portions of the court trial transcript be read to them. A juror can ask the judge for clarification of any rule of law or aspect of the trial. All of these communications are generally conducted in the presence of the lawyers for each side, or at least with their knowledge and consent.

During deliberations, you will be exposed to a lot of different opinions from other jurors. Each person will have their own beliefs and ideas. There may be someone on the jury who insists that the defendant is innocent due to one small, inconsequential factor, but they are ignoring the totality of the evidence. Not everything will always be fully explained. You can make sure that if one of your fellow jurors is stuck on one factor that they think does not seem to fit, they have that element explained to them by submitting a question to the judge. These issues should be a major concern in the scenario of the crime, not just a minor element.

No one on a jury should be on a mission looking for doubt. That is not the purpose of jury deliberations. The mission of your jury is to find the truth.

There may be a self-righteous juror who is hell-bent on acquittal no matter what. They may use the excuse that they are not convinced beyond a reasonable doubt, or they may state that the prosecution has not proven their case. If this is the case with multiple jurors, they may have a valid point, and it is best to consider their input. If it is only one or two jurors and their position does not seem to be based upon any solid evidence, you might want to lay out all the evidence from your "evidence tower." Try to help them understand that we can't know everything about the crime, and we must come to a rational and reasonable conclusion.

Regarding the prosecution's failure to prove its case, this is a highly subjective and potentially dangerous position. It must be a position that is based upon solid objections to the evidence presented and not just an unsupported opinion. "Well, I just think they haven't proven the case," should not be acceptable.

There may also be a situation where one juror does not believe the prosecution's scenario of how the crime happened. That does not automatically mean that the defendant is innocent. The prosecution's premise may be only one hypothesis to answer the questions posed by the evidence. There may be others that fit the circumstances revealed by the presentation of witnesses. As a juror, you do not have to accept the prosecution's scenario completely. The task is to evaluate the evidence and, if necessary, fill in your own sequence of events.

The system relies on reasonable people being able to put two and two together and extrapolate from specific facts the total of all the evidence to decide the defendant's guilt or innocence.

For example, the case is about a shooting. The defendant has argued with the victim in the past, the gun at the scene belongs to the defendant, the bullet matches that gun, and the defendant does not have a solid alibi for the time. However, no one actually saw him do it. There are no witnesses to it, and the defense may argue that this raises some reasonable doubt. However, the facts in this case lead us to conclude that it's beyond a reasonable doubt that the defendant committed the crime.

In some instances, the court may deem that the jury you are on is sequestered. Sequestered means that instead of going home at the end of the day, jurors stay in hotels, where their access to other people and the news is limited. The purpose is to prevent jurors from hearing information about the trial that wasn't presented in court, so they are not influenced. This is important because jurors must make their decisions based only on what they've heard during the trial.

Be aware that if jury deliberations take some time,

there may be jurors who want to finish so they can return home and be with their families, especially if you have been sequestered. You may have to hold the line and keep the jury on track.

Once all the evidence has been reviewed, the foreperson will ask for a vote. If a consensus is achieved from the vote, then the verdict is delivered to the court.

Verdict

To reach a verdict, the jury foreperson must have polled all the jurors, and the jurors have come to a consensus. The foreperson then notes the results and informs the bailiff. The bailiff will then give the verdict to the judge. Usually, but not always, the foreperson will read the verdict to the court.

Jury Is Dismissed

Now that you have been dismissed from the jury, you can use all of the problem-solving, critical thinking, and decision-making skills you have learned here in your regular life.

Within this book, you have been presented with several tips for jurors to detect suspicious behaviors of attorneys, but they can also be used when confronted by suspicious people in your life.

You can use the skills developed in this book in the real world to help you avoid being taken advantage of by scammers, in person or online, and by other unscrupulous people. One of the most common ways these skills can be used is when ferreting out fraudsters who are trying to get you to give them money.

You can recognize Semantic Infiltration when a family member or co-worker is trying to minimize the effect of something by using softer, milder words about an incident. "I just barely brushed against it, and it fell over and broke into a million pieces." Or "I really didn't mean anything by that statement."

You can use the techniques in this book to spot Gaslighting when a sibling or family member is trying to get you to believe something that you know didn't happen. They keep telling you that you were the one who spilled grandma's cranberry sauce all over the kitchen at Thanksgiving when you were eight. Or a significant other keeps telling you that you spent the last of the money in the checking account, making you question your spending habits.

You will know how to recognize The Hammer in action when a co-worker, or perhaps your boss, is slamming their hand down on the conference table or making a lot of verbal protestations as a deflection when it looks like they are wrong.

You now have the ability to identify Belief Speaking when a roommate, classmate, or co-worker is telling you a story and presenting it with a lot of "facts" in a frank manner, but you believe it is all made up. You can learn to cut through the noise presented as facts by a "sincere" but overly confident person.

You will be able to determine if your family member or maybe even your landlord is using a "look here, not there distraction to try to get you away from the issue at hand. They may bring up something that you or someone else did to try to direct you away from the real issue.

You will be able to recognize Superior Qualification syndrome when a classmate, co-worker, or even a roommate with a seemingly lot of credentials is stating something, perhaps a solution to a problem, but it just doesn't sound right to you, especially if the solution is slightly or entirely out of their area of expertise.

You can now distinguish when your children or siblings give you the SEDI defense, "Someone else did it, not me." Or say, "I don't know who did that, but it wasn't me," and you recognize they are just deflecting.

You might now be able to recognize when your family, children, co-workers, boss, or roommate is using one of these or other specious techniques to create Reasonable Doubt about some issue you are involved in. They might use multiple techniques to confuse the issue to try to confound and disorient you, but you will be able to recognize what they are trying to do.

You will recognize when a roommate is trying to explain why they downed the last bit of that drink and put the container back in the fridge, and they blame it on the devil or some mystical entity as a reason or excuse, saying, "The devil made me do it."

You will know when a person is playing the Rambo Lawyer, the person who uses a scorched earth method of dealing with problems, where everyone is persecuted for only one person's mistake or misstep in the office or even the classroom.

You can now recognize Bushwacking when your family or co-worker "suspect" has poisoned the family "jury pool" by getting to them first and making their own assertions outside of discussions with you. Or when they are using Bushwacking to tell a story to your co-workers to set up a fictional scenario where you messed up, instead of them, on that project.

Good luck in the jury room and out in the world.

Acknowledgments

I would like to acknowledge the great people at Genius Books for all their work on this project. I would also like to acknowledge my friend, fellow writer and editor, Rick Henning for his enthusiasm and support. We have both testified in court and recognize the tactics in this book.

Made in the USA
Monee, IL
04 November 2026

67387337R10085